International Political Economy Series

General Editor: **Timothy M. Shaw**, Professor of Political Science and International Development Studies, Dalhousie University, Halifax, Nova Scotia

Titles include:

Leslie Elliott Armijo (*editor*)
FINANCIAL GLOBALIZATION AND DEMOCRACY IN EMERGING MARKETS

Robert Boardman
THE POLITICAL ECONOMY OF NATURE
Environmental Debates and the Social Sciences

Gordon Crawford
FOREIGN AID AND POLITICAL REFORM
A Comparative Analysis of Democracy Assistance and Political Conditionality

Matt Davies
INTERNATIONAL POLITICAL ECONOMY AND MASS COMMUNICATION
IN CHILE
National Intellectuals and Transnational Hegemony

Martin Doornbos
INSTITUTIONALIZING DEVELOPMENT POLICIES AND RESOURCE
STRATEGIES IN EASTERN AFRICA AND INDIA
Developing Winners and Losers

Fred P. Gale
THE TROPICAL TIMBER TRADE REGIME

Mary Ann Haley
FREEDOM AND FINANCE
Democratization and Institutional Investors in Developing Countries

Keith M. Henderson and O. P. Dwivedi (*editors*)
BUREAUCRACY AND THE ALTERNATIVES IN WORLD PERSPECTIVES

Jomo K.S. and Shyamala Nagaraj (*editors*)
GLOBALIZATION VERSUS DEVELOPMENT

Angela W. Little
LABOURING TO LEARN
Towards a Political Economy of Plantations, People and Education
in Sri Lanka

John Loxley (*editor*)
INTERDEPENDENCE, DISEQUILIBRIUM AND GROWTH
Reflections on the Political Economy of North–South Relations at the
Turn of the Century

Don D. Marshall
CARIBBEAN POLITICAL ECONOMY AT THE CROSSROADS
NAFTA and Regional Developmentalism

Susan M. McMillan
FOREIGN DIRECT INVESTMENT IN THREE REGIONS OF THE SOUTH AT
THE END OF THE TWENTIETH CENTURY

James H. Mittelman and Mustapha Pasha (*editors*)
OUT FROM UNDERDEVELOPMENT
Prospects for the Third World (Second Edition)

Lars Rudebeck, Olle Törnquist and Virgilio Rojas (*editors*)
DEMOCRATIZATION IN THE THIRD WORLD
Concrete Cases in Comparative and Theoretical Perspective

Howard Stein (*editor*)
ASIAN INDUSTRIALIZATION AND AFRICA
Studies in Policy Alternatives to Structural Adjustment

International Political Economy Series
Series Standing Order ISBN 0–333–71708–2 hardcover
(*outside North America only*)

You can receive future titles in this series as they are published by placing a standing order.
Please contact your bookseller or, in case of difficulty, write to us at the address below with
your name and address, the title of the series and the ISBN quoted above.

Customer Services Department, Macmillan Distribution Ltd, Houndmills, Basingstoke,
Hampshire RG21 6XS, England

Freedom and Finance

Democratization and Institutional Investors in Developing Countries

Adjunct Professor
Fairfield University
Connecticut
USA

First published 2001 by
PALGRAVE
Houndmills, Basingstoke, Hampshire RG21 6XS and
175 Fifth Avenue, New York, N. Y. 10010
Companies and representatives throughout the world

PALGRAVE is the new global academic imprint of
St. Martin's Press LLC Scholarly and Reference Division and
Palgrave Publishers Ltd (formerly Macmillan Press Ltd).

ISBN 0–333–91448–1

This book is printed on paper suitable for recycling and
made from fully managed and sustained forest sources.

A catalogue record for this book is available
from the British Library.

Library of Congress Cataloging-in-Publication Data
Haley, Mary Ann, 1962–
    Freedom and finance : democratization and institutional
    investors in developing countries / Mary Ann Haley.
        p. cm. — (International political economy series)
    Includes bibliographical references and index.
    ISBN 0–333–91448–1
    1. Institutional investments—Developing countries.
    2. Investments, Foreign—Developing countries. 3. Democracy—
    –Developing countries. 4. Capitalism—Developing countries.
    I. Title. II. Series.
    HG5993 .H354 2000
    332.67'314'091724—dc21
                                                    00–053066

10   9   8   7   6   5   4   3   2   1
10 09 08 07 06 05 04 03 02 01

Printed and bound in Great Britain by
Antony Rowe Ltd, Chippenham, Wiltshire

For Zoë

Contents

List of Tables

List of Figures

Acknowledgements

I am grateful to those readers who offered not only their comments and suggestions but also their support and encouragement. These include Leslie Elliot Armijo, Bill Clark, Youssef Cohen, Tim Mitchell and Adam Przeworski. Thanks are also due to Robert Keohane, Birol Yesilada and Steve Smith for their comments on previous drafts. In addition to this helpful advice, I was lucky enough to be blessed with a father, George Haley, and an aunt, Patricia Haley Gibson, who were willing to read and make editorial suggestions on the manuscript. In addition, I would like to give a special thanks to T. M. Farmiloe for his enthusiasm and support in the early stages of this project and to Ann Marangos for her very valuable assistance in editing the book.

List of Abbreviations

ADR	American Depository Receipts
BEMI	Barings Emerging Markets Index
CMO	Collateralized Mortgage Obligations
CPC	Communist Party of Vietnam
EAFE	Europe, Australia, and the Far East
EMC	Emerging Market Country
EMFI	Emerging Markets Free Index
EMH	Efficient Market Hypothesis
EMT	Efficient Market Theory
EOI	Export-Oriented Industrialization
ESAF	Enhanced Structural Adjustment Facility
FAT	Authentic Labor Front
FID	Foreign Investment Directorate
FDI	Foreign Direct Investment
G-7	Group of Seven
GAB	General Arrangements to Borrow
GATT	General Agreement on Tariffs and Trade
GDP	Gross Domestic Product
GDR	Global Depository Receipt
GDS	Gross Domestic Savings
HIID	Harvard Institute of International Development
ICM	International Capital Markets
IFC	International Finance Corporation
IFCG	International Finance Corporation Global (Index)
IFCI	International Finance Corporation Investable (Index)
IIF	Institute of International Finance
ILBE	Institute for Law-Based Economy
IMF	International Monetary Fund
IPO	International Public Offering
ISG	International Securities Group
LDC	Less Developed Country
MAI	Multilateral Agreement on Investment
MDB	Multilateral Development Bank
MIGA	Multilateral Investment Guarantee Agency

MNC	Multinational Corporation
MSCI	Morgan Stanley Capital International (Index)
NAB	New Arrangements to Borrow
NGO	Non-Governmental Organization
NIC	Newly Industrializing Country
NRF	Net Resource Flow
ODA	Official Development Assistance
ODF	Official Development Finance
OECD	Organization of Economic Cooperation and Development
PRD	Partido Revolucionario Democratico
RPC	Russian Privatization Center
SAP	Structural Adjustment Program
SEC	Securities and Exchange Commission
S&P	Standard and Poor's
SOE	State-Owned Enterprise
TNC	Transnational Corporation
USAID	United States Agency for International Development

List of Appendixes

1
Introduction: Private Investment Flows and Institutional Investors

The nineteenth-century ideal of erecting a world based on the unencumbered operation of a free market has reemerged and has permeated the public policies and politics at the turn of the millennium. Akin to its role in the nineteenth century, international finance is playing a central role in the promulgation of the free market norm. The developing countries in Asia, Latin America and Africa are perhaps the most affected by this resurgence of liberalism and the demands of international finance. The conventional means of attracting capital into developing countries shifted rapidly from pledging allegiances to one of the cold war rivals to marketing the nation-state to the world's financiers. Once a strategic geopolitical position could have ensured a consistent flow of assistance; now an economic policy, based on deregulation, privatization, and stabilization, is the path to equity. Instead of catering to the governments and international institutions of industrialized countries, leaders in developing countries realize that the power of the purse lies with private institutional investors. The political and social ramification of this change in finance sourcing for developing countries has yet to be explored fully. The goal of this book is to further the on-going debate about the relationship between liberalization and democratization, and to challenge some convenient assumptions about markets that do not hold in the current emerging financial markets. Close observation of institutional investors – those controlling the majority of capital flowing into developing countries today – draws into question the relative freedom and fairness of these markets.

1

The new emerging financial markets, occurring simultaneously within the global wave of neoliberal reform, may also have an impact on democratic transitions and consolidations. The neoliberal reform wave, the mix of market-oriented economic reforms coined by John Williamson as the 'Washington consensus,' consists of trade liberalization, exchange rate stabilization, state-owned enterprise privatization, and the reduction of government expenditures. As Paul Krugman puts it 'Governments that had spent half a century pursuing statist, protectionist policies suddenly got free market religion' (Krugman, 1995). The impetus for these reforms was the prospect of reeling in investments. Again, Krugman suggests that if one could 'find a country that has done these things, ... there one may confidently expect to realize high returns on investment' (Krugman, 1995). Demonstrating the non-competitive and inefficient elements within the emerging financial markets challenges the neo-liberal tenet that the market is an abstract entity that serves as simply an apolitical mechanism for distributing goods within society. Instead, these markets do not function by an invisible hand, I argue, but are controlled by the visible hands of institutional investors. The concentration of assets and coordination among these investors indicates that this portion of the expansion of neoliberalism does not necessarily engender the market of 'faceless stock, bond and currency traders sitting behind computer screens all over the globe' popularly portrayed by Friedman (1999). Furthermore, in light of the amount of control these institutional investors have over the resources flowing to developing countries, their preferences now serve as guideposts for those countries wanting to attract private capital. This book explores whether the frequently expressed criteria, that is stability and growth, for selecting a country in which to invest, adversely affects political democracy. This combination, the distortion of fair market principles allowing institutional investors to accrue considerable power, plus the subsequent potency of their preferences due to this power, suggests that within this most recent wave of democratization lies a countervailing force. This force is a financial market that empowers money managers who value stability and growth over political democracy.

By examining the new regime in which private investors increasingly exercise the power attached to the control of capital, we arrive at an analysis that probes the relationship between capital sourcing, and political and economic transformations. The scope of this book is not to explore all the political and economic phenomena resulting from financial globalization, but rather to focus on institutional investors' norms and practices, and how these can influence developing countries. The central question is how institutional investors impact democratization in developing countries. Through testing for coordination and other violations of fair market principles, the analysis first establishes the viability of institutional investors as political actors. If institutional investor action is coordinated, then they are an organized unit within the international system, and their objectives and practices should perhaps be held to a scrutiny similar to the International Monetary Fund (IMF), World Bank, or other financial development institutions. Therefore, a first step in showing linkage between private investment and domestic political and economic changes in developing countries is to demonstrate investor coordination – their capacity to function as a system within the international system. Once coordination has been established, the next task is to investigate their preferences and to explore how these are expressed in the system of international finance. If institutional investors are influencing the politics in developing countries, as foreign aid donors and other international entities have done in the past, what type of organization, norms, and methods of communication do they utilize to achieve this? Are there signaling devices and/or codes of ethics which structure and reproduce the systems in which they operate? If there is imperfect competition in the international markets for developing country equities, what are the potential effects on democracy? What are the channels in which investors communicate and what are the norms, categories, and results produced by this organizational system? In addition, in what ways can individual investors influence policies in emerging market countries? These questions will be addressed in the following format.

The book is divided into six chapters. Chapter 1 begins by reviewing some of the literature, which helps inform the question of a connection between institutional investor capital and politics in developing countries. The second half of Chapter 1 describes the shift from official development assistance to private finance; it differentiates forms of investment and discusses the growing importance of finance capital and the role of institutional investors in the emerging markets. Chapter 2 establishes institutional investors as political actors in the international system by answering two questions. First, do large investors possess undue influence other investors and the market? Secondly, do emerging market investors act independently of one another in response to certain political and economic phenomena in developing countries, or; is there a departure from efficient and fair market distribution? Here, the international market for developing country equities is investigated for violations of fair market practices. If institutional investors are to be considered political actors in the international system, it is first necessary to determine if their actions are coordinated, or if they are responding independently to macroeconomic and risk data. This section does not differentiate between intentional or unintentional coordination nor does it explore the signals around which investors may coordinate. Rather, it seeks only to uncover the existence of a violation of the widespread neo-liberal premise that financial markets will allocate capital fairly. Once it is shown that institutional investors do coordinate and have influence over pricing, then the focus turns towards shared investor preferences for emerging market countries and the types of coordination that take place.

Chapter 3 explores the criteria used by investors to choose a country for their portfolios. In this chapter, the preferences of institutional investors are uncovered through a survey of various mediums in which investors have made known what they think to be the most important determinants of a worthy emerging market investment. Chapter 4 shows how institutional investors help produce the norms of the global financial system that ultimately benefits them. This chapter focuses exclusively on structural factors that are external to developing countries. The chapter is organized into levels of coordination that take place among investors when common goals and outcomes result from varying degrees of cohesion over policy direction in developing countries. Chapter 5 outlines how institutional investors attempt to exercise their power as political actors in developing countries. By drawing parallels between domestic and international investor activism, this chapter illustrates the growing trend of institutional investors' governance in emerging markets. Chapter 6 focuses on the political impact that occurs as a result of coordination and activism on the part of institutional investors. It questions whether the emergence of financial markets, a staple of late twentieth century economic reform, has a positive effect on civil liberties and/or political rights in developing countries. It examines the impact institutional investors may have on democracy, either as a group or as individual investors working according to the rules of thumb which guide international finance.

Theoretical perspectives on development and global finance

Key to economic development in developing countries has been the ability to maintain a flow of capital into the infrastructures and industries targeted for expansion. However, the sources and method by which capital flows into developing countries is not often found in political science inquiries. More specifically, few theories about political and economic development have included international finance in their equations of freedom and growth. Theories about advanced capitalism most often conceive the international flow of capital as an abstract process in which rational actors seek to maximize returns for investments within a global marketplace. The abstract market and the reduction of investors to rational actors with homogenized preferences obfuscate the power and specific preferences of the individuals at the source of international financial flows. However, a few scholars of capitalism have contributed to the understanding of these large money managers' potential impact on developing countries' politics. For instance, the spread of liberalism today is often compared with the economic system that preceded the two world wars (Arrighi, 1994: 71; Lash and Urry, 1994; Wachtel, 1988). At the end of World War II many scholars sought to uncover the systemic causes of World Wars I and II. Two schools of thought emerged representing the liberal and socialist politics of the time. Scholars such as F.A. Hayek defended free market liberalism and blamed the demise of nineteenth century peace on the anti-democratic strains he perceived embedded in socialism. Critics of the free market system, such as Karl Polyani, blamed *laissez-faire* ideology as the underlying cause of war. Polyani, in particular, provides reference points about past practices of international financiers in developing countries, particularly during the century before World War I.

Giovanni Arrighi presents another image of advanced capitalism by extending the historical insights of Ferdinand Braudel's observations on the mechanisms of capitalism and market economies.

Against those theorists claiming capitalism has no order, Arrighi argues that capitalism is indeed organized. He provides historical evidence of a cyclical system that demonstrates capital's inherent motion to move from mobility to rigidity and back again to mobility. Using the examples of the Genoese, Dutch, and British hegemonies of capital, Arrighi shows that each eventually moved into the position of financier, and away from its industrial power base. Indeed, the coveted position for those possessing capital power is to move to a position of greater flexibility, and thereby gain the advantage of moving more easily from the less profitable to the more lucrative. Arrighi argues against those seeing flexible specialization (Piore and Sable, 1984; Sable and Zeitlin, 1985; Hirst and Zeitlin, 1991) and flexible accumulation (Harvey, 1989) as a novelty resulting from the 1970s crisis of the international economic order. On the contrary, Arrighi sees 'flexibility' as an inherent goal of capitalism all along. The most recent change of capitalism towards more flexibility is simply the penultimate part of a system cycle featuring US hegemony. Thus, the advent of institutional investors' power marks the deepening of hegemony rather than a freeing.

Susan Strange also provides provocative commentary on the world financial systems in the second edition of her work *Casino Capitalism* (1997). Especially insightful for understanding the movements of portfolio capital today are Strange's comments about the growth of the financial futures trading markets and their impact on international financial flows. Strange observes the increase of uncertainty in the global economy as the 'number of volatile variables in the monetary and financial structure of the international political economy multiplied' (119). This uncertainty is what precipitated the great increase of trading in financial futures, an activity geared towards the reduction of risk. That response, according to Strange, began 'a vicious cycle of risk-averse responses, which in turn have added to the volatility of the variables and consequently to the general sense of confusion and the faltering confidence in the viability of the global financial system' (119). Prophetic words in light of the crash of the Asian stock markets in 1997, due in a large part to the trading in financial futures.

In addition, the tremendous change in the means of acquiring capital in the 1980s is left out of most discussions on economic development and democracy. Through an examination of this shift to private financing and the accompanying politics of investor-driven international financing, insight can be gained into the interrelationship between democracy and economic growth. Theorists linking economic reforms and democracy in particular can benefit from knowledge of institutional investor's influence over developing country reforms. Some important studies that focus on the interrelationship between reforms and democracy include Bollen (1990), Arat (1991), Barro (1994), Przeworski (1993), Burkhart and Lewis-Beck (1994), Gasiorowski (1994), Haggard and Webb (1994), and Bhalla (1994).

Recently a relatively small group of scholars began looking at the relationship between the 1980s and 1990s increase of private finance to developing countries and the impact this has had on democratization. An eclectic mix of representatives from the international finance community, international relations, comparative politics, and economics has produced a small body of literature that marks the beginning of the study of this relationship. Within this body of work, several case studies stand out for their contribution in understanding the particular changes that have taken place because of this new finance capital influx.[1] However, even in this more recent work, the role of the institutional investor is understated. Some of the primary contributors to this newer body of work are discussed in later pages.

Private investment flows and the shift to private finance

In the last two decades of the millennium, a significant shift occurred in the composition of capital flows to developing countries. First, official development financing (ODF) declined significantly. After a 92 per cent increase, from 1984 to 1995, from US$33.4 billion to US$64.2 billion, ODF dropped to only US$4.7 billion in 1998, a decrease of 1,266 per cent. Secondly, private financing increased dramatically, from US$35.6 billion in 1984 to US$165.5 billion in 1998, an increase of 365 per cent (World Bank, 1999). In 1984, official development finance made up the majority of funds flowing to developing countries, with nearly 50 per cent of the total net long-term resource flows (see Table 1.2). By 1996, ODF provided only 1 per cent of these flows and private financing comprised

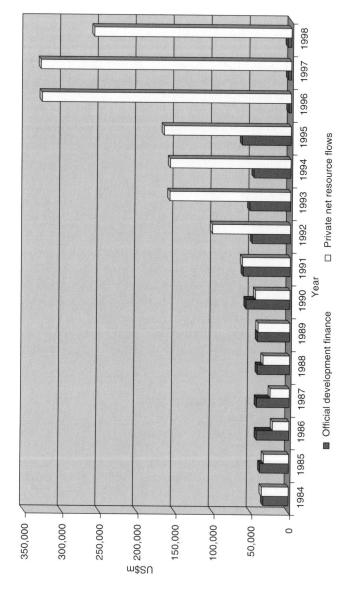

Figure 1.1 Net long-term resource flows to developing countries: official and private, 1984–98
Source: Global Development Finance on CD-ROM, 1999.

99 per cent of the capital coming into developing countries (see Table 1.2). Figure 1.1 highlights the transformation in the composition of capital flows to developing countries.

The central difference between private investment and official development finance is the explicit expectation for a rate of return. However, various types of private investments differ significantly. For instance, it is important to differentiate between portfolio equity, bonds, foreign direct investment, and commercial bank loans. Each holds a specific set of expectations, manifested in the actions of the controlling investor. Foreign direct investment (FDI), for example, is usually assumed to be longer term and that investors will take an active role through forms of ownership, joint ventures, or limited partnerships. Portfolio investments, or stocks and bonds, in comparison, are often shorter term and are much more flexible, and thus, volatile. However, even within the category of portfolio investments, there are significant differences between instruments.

The following descriptions of different types of capital sources are important not only to understanding the possible differences in preferences that may arise from them but also to uncover the widespread trend of the spread of portfolio type investments. Not only has portfolio capital increased as its own separate category of investment but it has also contributed to the decrease of other types of financing. FDI as well as commercial bank loans are increasingly utilizing new financing methods grounded in portfolio equity arrangements.

Portfolio investments: stocks and bonds

Private investment into developing countries has increased overall, but the fastest growing category of investment has been portfolio investments and equity financing. The total amount of resources from the international capital markets (both portfolio and private loans) reached over US$203 billion in 1996, an increase of 677 per cent from 1984. However, as Table 1.1 indicates, total portfolio investment, or stocks and bonds, has increased from US$33 million in 1984 to US$102.7 billion in 1996, an increase of 311,112 per cent! As Figure 1.2 illustrates, the total from the international capital markets made up 66 per cent of all private investment flows to developing countries in 1996, while official development finance

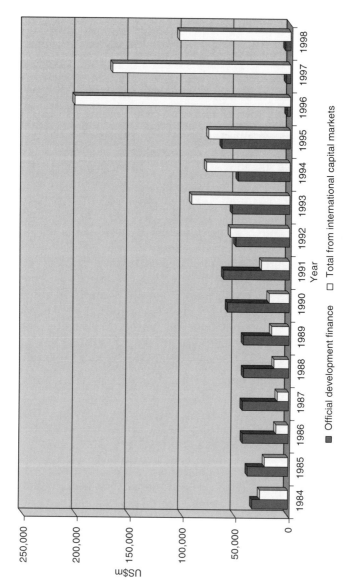

Figure 1.2 Capital flows to developing countries: official development finance and international capital markets, 1984–98

Source: Global Development Finanace, CD-ROM, 1999.

Table 1.1 Net resource flows to developing countries, 1984–98 (US$m)

	Year														
	1984	1985	1986	1987	1988	1989	1990	1991	1992	1993	1994	1995	1996	1997	1998
Official Development Finance	33,437	37,833	42,877	43,352	42,428	42,556	57,944	61,770	50,305	53,910	48,600	64,200	3,220	3,910	4,790
ODA	21,177	26,619	29,318	33,497	36,391	36,934	44,868	47,802	43,050	42,414	44,586.2	44,700	40,010	33,400	32,700
Non-concessionary loans	12,261	11,215	13,559	9,854	6,036	5,623	13,076	13,967	7,256	11,497	9,813.3	8,800	−7,900	5,700	15,200
International capital markets	26,133	21,962	11,496	10,600	13,838	16,249	18,835	26,127	55,649	92,588	78,700	76,800	203,000	167,514	105,111
Total Portfolio Investment	33	5,749	1,364	1,802	3,985	8,770	7,193	20,034	27,116	88,980	67,100	55,700	102,700	62,214	47,111
Bonds	−117	5,611	758	1,041	2,889	5,285	3,419	12,482	12,944	42,046	32,200	33,700	53,500	42,600	30,200
Portfolio equity	150	138	606	761	1,096	3,486	3,774	7,552	14,172	46,934	34,900	22,000	49,200	19,614	16,911
FDI	9,437	11,330	10,253	14,576	21,182	25,687	26,712	36,810	47,076	66,614	80,100	90,300	126,400	163,400	155,000
Private Loans	26,101	16,214	10,132	8,799	9,853	7,479	11,642	6,093	28,533	3,608	11,600	21,100	100,300	105,300	58,000
Commercial banks	21,159	8,495	3,259	2,993	7,317	866	120	3,968	12,836	−2,200	9,200	17,100	43,700	60,100	25,100
Suppliers	775	−244	829	991	−886	1,073	7,301	−2,168	−16	1,994	2,400	4,000	na	na	na
Other private	4,167	7,963	6,045	4,815	3,422	5,540	4,221	4,292	15,713	3,813	3,700	1,000	3,000	2,600	2,700
Aggregate Net Resource Flows	69,008	71,125	64,625	68,537	77,447	84,493	103,490	124,706	153,031	213,112	207,400	231,300	308,000	338,100	275,000

Source: Global Development Finance on CD-ROM, 1999.

Table 1.2   Percentage breakdown of net resource flows (NRFs) to developing countries, 1984–98 (Percentage from ODA, ICM and FDI)

Year	ODA (% of NRF)	ICM (% of NRF)	FDI (% of NRF)
1984	0.48	0.38	0.14
1985	0.53	0.31	0.16
1986	0.66	0.18	0.16
1987	0.63	0.15	0.21
1988	0.55	0.18	0.27
1989	0.5	0.19	0.3
1990	0.56	0.18	0.26
1991	0.5	0.21	0.3
1992	0.33	0.36	0.31
1993	0.25	0.43	0.31
1994	0.23	0.38	0.39
1995	0.28	0.33	0.39
1996	0.01	0.66	0.41
1997	0.01	0.5	0.48
1998	0.02	0.38	0.56

comprised only 1 per cent of the total net long term flows (see also Table 1.2). The 1997 Asian Crisis decreased dramatically the overall portfolio flows to emerging markets in 1997 and 1998. However, this decline appears to be only a temporary slowing of the overall trend towards heavier reliance on portfolio capital. As Table 1.2 indicates, in 1998, the international capital markets still comprised 38 per cent of the total net resource flows to developing countries while official aid and credit make up only 2 per cent of the total. FDI, primarily financed through the international capital markets, comprised the remaining percentage.

Developing countries that are frequent recipients of these new portfolio flows are commonly referred to as 'the emerging markets'. The term 'emerging market' originated in 1986 when the World Bank's International Finance Corporation was given the task of creating a fund for capital market development for developing countries. The success of this fund is now a part of financial history. The reasons for its success, as well as the subsequent take-off of copycat funds, can be attributed to three essential factors. First, the volume of capital accumulation that lays in institutional funds such as insurance companies and pension plans had been growing rapidly since the inception of the postwar economic system in the industrialized countries. New venues for investment were needed as interest rates rose and returns on investment in the developed world became less lucrative. Secondly, the rapid growth in East Asia produced an investment opportunity that provided investors an alternative for international diversification and risk reduction. The subsequent high rate of returns of some of these Asia funds spurred the growth of many other 'emerging market' funds. Thirdly, as developing countries across the globe witnessed the success of the East Asian tigers, development schemes based on aspects of their policy successes were promoted through international agencies like the IMF. This blueprint for growth, which prioritized austerity programs, privatization, and exports, had the added benefit of being highly attractive to foreign investors.[2] The absence of a visible alternative, combined with the apparent success of the East Asian development model, produced a rather straightforward recipe for economic reform. The installation of a plethora of new financial infrastructures accompanied the privatizations and export-oriented strategies. Stock markets began opening up in remote corners of the world and this new category for investments, emerging markets, expanded as an option for institutional investors.

There are two main divisions within portfolio investments, stocks (equities), and bonds. Within these categories, there are also a growing number of derivative markets that trade options on particular emerging market stocks, and futures on emerging market currencies and commodities. The differences between these financial instruments can be significant and can vary from country to country. Portfolio equity, or the purchasing of shares of a particular corporation or project, usually requires the presence of a stock market where the shares can be traded. While the majority of emerging market equities is traded in the country where the corporation is domiciled, some larger corporations also issue depository receipts, such as American Depository Receipts (ADRs). This enables them to sell shares on foreign exchanges like the New York Stock Exchange. Portfolio equity is generally regarded as riskier than holding bonds and, traditionally has been considered a more aggressive growth investment strategy.

The issuing of bonds as a source of external financing is not a new phenomenon in global finance. Throughout the nineteenth century, London functioned as the primary financial center from which foreign government securities were sold. For instance, from 1822 to 1825, Latin American government bond issues comprised the largest portion of foreign government securities sold on the London Exchange.[3] In addition, from 1890 to 1929, bond financing was the predominant means by which developing countries received capital (Manzocchi, 1999). Developing countries borrowed at a discount from large banks and those banks then sold bonds on this debt to individual investors. Bond financing for developing countries was scarce following the crash of the New York Stock Exchange in 1929. It remained small until the restructuring of debt obligations through the Brady Plan in 1989.

The Brady Plan, guaranteeing bonds issued by debtor nations through US treasuries, provided the impetus for a substantial increase in developing country bond issues and consequently purchases by institutional investors in the 1990s. By 1995, 13 developing countries had issued Brady bonds with a cumulative face value of more than US$150 billion.[4] Because of the increasing bond issues and debt purchases by industrialized countries, the market for trading emerging market debt increased dramatically. From 1990 to 1993, the volume traded by the top ten debt traders doubled each year. By 1996, trading volume totaled over US$5.2 trillion (million million) a year (Eng *et al.*, 1998).

Either price or yield, or both attracts the bond purchaser, as it does the stock purchaser.[5] Their time horizons therefore, can vary considerably depending on their investment strategy and/or mandate. Bonds, traditionally long-term holds within the securities industry, are now often one of the most rapidly traded investments available. They can be traded in a fraction of a second, 24 hours a day, and demonstrate the same volatility as equities in the developing countries.

Commercial banks

Commercial banks have historically played a crucial role in external financing to developing countries. Following the crash of the New York Stock Exchange and the world economy in 1929, capital transfers from industrialized countries to developing ones mostly dried up until the 1960s. In the 1960s and 1970s, the ensuing capital flows to the developing countries were largely comprised of commercial bank loans and official development assistance. Banks accelerated their rate of lending to developing countries during this period for several reasons. Some of these reasons include the increased demand for development projects, the increased supply of lending capital derived from the new Euroloan markets, and the need to recycle the significant expansion of petrodollars. The 1970s provided some unique environmental factors that encouraged bank lending to developing countries at an unprecedented rate. By 1982, the debt crisis was apparent and banks, facing the risk of great losses, curtailed their lending practices to developing countries sharply. In the early 1980s, securities market lending began replacing more traditional forms of financing and rose from one-quarter to a nine-tenths share of foreign lending in the first half of the decade (Solomon, 1995: 439). Because of the debt crisis, commercial banks implemented new strategies and instruments to enable them better to hedge risk, as well as compete with investment and securities firms. These innovations are important in understanding the growth of portfolio-style investments to developing countries as commercial banks convert traditional lending practices into a more securities-based activity.

The nature of commercial bank lending has changed significantly over the last decade as well. The practice of securitizing loans has become an integral component of the banking business. Securitization involves the pooling together of loans for the purposes of resale, mainly through the issuance of particular types of securities. These securities, including collateralized mortgage obligations (CMOs), offer investors a relatively low risk investment that yields interest, making this an attractive fixed-income product. Securitization has dramatically increased the profitability of banks and has permanently altered conventional bank lending. The increase of the practice of securitization has also increased the amount of assets held as securities in the US and the amount of portfolio capital relative to bank-held assets.

In addition to the securitization of loans, legislation allowing banks to provide clients with stock and bond investing services has also increased the amount of capital held in securities and decreased the relative assets in traditional savings accounts. The lifting of some of the regulations of the Glass-Steagall Act has been central to this process. The purpose of Glass-Steagall Act of 1933, enacted after the 1929 crash, was to erect protective barriers between commercial banks, investment firms, and insurance companies in case of a crisis. More recently, it has been challenged by the 1993 Citicorp-Travelers Bill. The dismantling of Glass-Steagall, combined with the desire to compete globally against more integrated financial giants, has prompted banks and securities firms to forge new partnerships and mergers. This has created corporations of unprecedented assets. The union of Travelers Group, an owner of securities and insurance firms, and Citibank created Citigroup, the largest corporation in the world, as measured by assets. The addition of security advising and investment services to commercial banks undoubtedly increased the relative size of many banks. However, this move has also precipitated the spread of the allure of the stock market to many more people and thus added to the relative amount of assets held in portfolio capital versus traditional bank accounts.

Two other phenomena have diminished the power of traditional domestic bank lending as well as the power of national central banks. Intensive globalization has opened a plethora of international borrowing opportunities. The strength of the dollar and the US economy have increased the demand for imports and the outflow of dollars to other economies. This outflow has increased the liquidity in other parts of the globe and allowed other lending opportunities to emerge for the US population and its borrowing mentality. In addition, the US investor has increasingly preferred to put savings into the stock market and the relative share of US assets in banks has dropped significantly. In 1980 banks accounted for 56 per cent of financial assets in the US and by 1994 that percentage had dropped to 35 per cent (Melloan, 1996: A17). These upsurges in portfolio capital through the changes in banking practices have reduced the role of traditional bank lender and increased the power of portfolio capital within international finance.

The diminishing of the traditional banking relationship, combined with the new upsurge in other types of lending, has created a new environment in which new rules exist. Perhaps the most significant is the shortened time horizons of the lenders. At a conference on Latin American debt held in 1996, Eduardo Mansferrer of

Hamilton Bank commented on this phenomenon as he addresses some of economic problems of the region:

> In some of the crisis of the past, it is not always and automatically the borrowers fault. Sometimes the lenders are at fault too. Global capital markets are changing and an increasing amount of funds is being channeled outside regular commercial banking relationships. This new funds are only interested in short term gain, there is no long-term view (Morles, 1996).

These statements highlight the awareness of shortened time horizons as well as the culpability of lenders in this practice.

FDI and portfolio flows

FDI, the other major category that increased over the 1984–98 period, appears to have exceeded the international capital markets as the main supplier of capital to developing countries in 8 of the last 15 years. Following the Asian crisis in 1997, FDI made up 56 per cent of the total net resource flows (NRF) to less developed countries (LDCs) in 1998. However, FDI remained less than the total amount of portfolio investments and private bank loans in 1996, making up 41 per cent of the total flows to the international capital markets' 66 per cent (see Table 1.2). Given that FDI is usually longer term and more heavily regulated in terms of its ability to exit from the host country, foreign direct investors would seem to have the most incentive to influence the politics of developing countries. It could be argued that this would be the most logical category of investment to examine the impact this shift to private capital has made on democracy in developing countries.

However, the focus of this book will remain on financial market investments because traditional FDI is less important than portfolio capital in analysing private capital's impact on democratization in developing countries for four reasons. First, FDI is not new. Developing countries have courted this type of investment for centuries. Joint ventures and co-ownership are not a recent phenomenon and therefore have not qualitatively changed the political landscape in developing countries in the last decade.

Secondly, the increase in FDI is an anomaly and not a qualitative shift. What is new is the confluence of this increase with an increase in portfolio financing.[6] Normally, an increase in FDI would be accompanied by a decrease in bond financing, and conversely, a decrease in FDI would be accompanied by a surge in bond financing. The reasons for this anomaly suggest that the increase in FDI be treated as a blip rather than a qualitative shift in financing (IMF, 1995: 36). For instance, the wave of deregulation, debt relief, and privatization suggest that the new influx of FDI is simply a one-time shift in response to this wide-spread phenomena, and not a trend which will continue (Dooley, 1986; IMF, 1995). It is likely that FDI will decrease as the number of public enterprises available for privatization reach a plateau (IMF, 1995: 36). Another reason for the increase in FDI is the reinvestment of funds resulting from domestic growth within the recipient countries. Thus, FDI is in part dependent on economic expansion of the recipient countries. Since it costs investors less to reinvest funds than it does to raise them, reinvestment can be expected to be a relatively constant flow as long as the host economy expands and regulations do not change. For much of FDI, regulatory frameworks are already in place.

The third reason for the decline in importance of traditional forms of FDI is the composition of FDI is shifting to portfolio financing. Projects normally funded through FDI, in particular large infrastructure projects, are now increasingly financed through portfolio funds and bond issues. This fact implies that FDI is falling increasingly into the domain of the institutional portfolio investors. An example of this is the trend in financing infrastructure development projects, one of the largest areas of FDI. Touted as the 'next glamour investment' by one of the leading publications on FDI, infrastructure funds are growing rapidly in popularity among top institutional investors.[7] Christopher Perry reports that within three months, Global Power Investments, started by George Soros of Quantum Industrial Holdings, Gary Wendt of GE Capital, and the IFC, raised over US$450 million for investments in the power sector in emerging market countries. As Perry observes, this serves as an example of the expansion of individual institutional investors into emerging market projects:

> A somewhat incestuous jumble of money men, equipment suppliers and multilateral agencies are packaging a range of

multimillion dollar funds to invest in infrastructure projects around the world ...

and

The largest [infrastructure] funds are the creations of a veritable 'Who's Who' of American business ...

and

Some of the biggest names in the U.S. money business are behind a variety of new infrastructure funds ... (Perry, 1994: 20).

In spring 1994, estimates suggested that infrastructure funds received approximately US$4 billion in equity commitments.[8] Such projects, traditionally financed through FDI commercial bank loans, are particularly attractive to the largest institutional investors such as insurance companies and pension funds. Bond and equity financing on infrastructure projects typically offer less risk because of the availability of multilateral institution's risk insurance guarantees and repayment strategies based on user-fees.

Furthermore, even financing that falls under the category of 'FDI', is often backed by securitized loans, bond issues, or other types of portfolio-financing strategies. This distinction is not reflected in the current methods of accounting within institutions like the World Bank. The World Bank's statistics on FDI, found in the widely used Global Development Finance reports (previously World Debt Tables), are based on a definition that can include a high percentage of portfolio capital stocks as well:

an investment that is made to acquire a lasting management interest (usually 10 percent of voting stock) in an enterprise operating in a country other than that of the investor (defined according to residency), the investor's purpose being an effective voice in the management of the enterprise. It is the sum of equity capital, reinvestment of earnings, other long-term capital, and short-term capital as shown in the balance of payments (World Bank, 1999).

This definition means, for instance, that if a US institutional investor purchases more than 10 per cent of voting stock in a company in a developing country, this would be considered FDI. Contrary to the belief that FDI is only a 'long-term' investment, this definition includes short-term and equity capital. A representative at Morgan Stanley Dean Witter commented, 'In these emerging market countries it is very difficult for us *not* to own more than 10 per cent of a company.'[9]

Understandably, many emerging market countries are encouraging this trend by allowing portfolio type issues, such as Global Depository Receipts (GDRs), to be treated legally like FDI. India, for instance, allows Indian companies to raise equity capital for manufacturing needs like equipment and plant installations, as well as infrastructure projects in telecommunications, power, airports, and roads. Treating this equity capital as FDI eliminates investment ceilings for companies and allows foreign 'ownership' to exceed 51 per cent of a proposed plant or project (Andrapradesh web site, 1999: 1). East Asia, with some of the lowest rates of private financing for infrastructure projects, has also begun taking steps to expand portfolio financing for airports, roads, power plants, etc. For instance, China has begun to 'pool' assets from its existing power plants with asset needs for new projects in order to attract 'fixed income investors' (Mody and Walton, 1998: 23). Recommendations for raising private capital for infrastructure include increasing the utilization of domestic stock markets and expanding the issuance of bonds for infrastructure projects (Mody and Walton, 1998: 25). Projects like the Ras Laffan Liquefied Natural Gas project in Qatar, is an example of bond financing – with a US$1.2 billion bond issue offered to investors in the project. Classifying this portfolio financing as 'FDI' can contribute to the underestimation of portfolio financing and the overestimation of FDI.

In addition to the entrance of institutional investors in FDIs, another increasingly popular trend is for large equipment manufacturers, engineering firms, and corporations involved in the proposed project, to act as financiers. Given the size of some of these companies it is not surprising that in the 1980s these companies started developing their own methods of financing, which end up acting much like portfolio flows. Institutional investors themselves make up the other large group of participants in FDI. As mentioned in the above paragraphs, the top money managers are becoming increasingly interested in FDI and are taking an active stance in creating funds to channel into these enterprises.

The fourth reason to keep the emphasis on portfolio financing is the argument derived from Hirshman's *Exit, Voice, and Loyalty* (1970).[10] This theory contends that although it is more difficult for foreign direct investors to move assets, such as a copper mine, than it is for a bond traders, this quicker exit ability enhances the credibility of the bond trader's threat. Hence, rulers can in fact feel more constrained by this more credible threat of exit. Kingstone (1999) and Stone (1999) support this theory in their analysis of the responsiveness to investors by the Brazilian and Russian leaders, respectively.

Derivative markets and currency trading

As emerging markets increase their market capitalization and their financial infrastructures expand, the trading of derivatives becomes more common. The level of derivatives trading – or those secondary markets that allow investors to hedge their risks with, or speculate on, the price of stocks, commodities, currencies, and other securities – can often be a sign of a country's financial market maturity.[11] Emerging market derivatives are in relative infancy, and although interesting, have much less impact on developing countries than industrialized countries' derivatives. In particular, the activities of currency speculators have had a tremendous impact on the economies of LDCs.

Currency speculators, often the catalysts for devaluation as they gamble on the directions of economies and the actions of politicians, can be seen as a particular kind of institutional investor. Hedge-fund managers do not buy directly into any one corporation through stock, but rather invest in the expectation of a country's success or failure. Hedge funds, utilized by multinational corporations to reduce their risk exposure to foreign currencies, have increased dramatically in this era of globalization. The 1998 demise of Long-term Capital Corporation revealed the extent to which even large securities firms relied on the expertise of currency traders to cover their international exposures. The growth of these hedge funds began in the 1970s as the amount traded in financial futures surpassed the amount traded in commodities. These funds, although primarily for large investors, are also increasingly marketed to smaller investors as vehicles for speculation rather than hedging. George Soros, founder of the Soros fund and perhaps the most well-known hedge fund expert, is an example of the success that currency trading has had and the subsequent power such funds can wield in the developing world.[12] As the Asian crisis has demonstrated, the impact the derivatives market, in particular currency trading, has had on developing countries can be profound. However, even with the enormous suffering caused by the crashes of many emerging market currencies in the late nineties, the new system for capital distribution to developing countries remains intact. Ironically, the economic crises wrought by the new system governing capital distribution has deepened the need for those countries in crisis to abide more fully by the rules set by those investors in part responsible for their crashes.

Conclusions

This chapter has outlined some of the trends in international global finance and how many of these trends involve the increase of more mobile, or as Arrighi suggests, flexible, capital. The decreases in official development assistance and traditional bank lending combined with the enormous upsurge in the use of port-folio capital for financing has led to changes in the fundamentals governing the system of capital distribution. In addition, the increased speed and proliferation of portfolio capital into traditional forms of financing like FDI and commercial bank lending, has deepened the reconfiguration of the global financial system over the last 15 years. Moreover, as financial globalization expands, currency trading becomes increasingly popular for those wanting to minimize their international exposure, as well as those wanting to profit from predicting the political and economic futures of nations. The success of the US stock market in the 1990s has further cemented the growing importance of portfolio capital as a potential means of financing. Small and large investors increasingly utilize equities as a means to grow their nest eggs and corporate accounts. Today it is rare to hear a television or radio newscast that does not report the closing daily numbers for the Dow Jones Industrial Average or the NASDAQ composite. Moreover, as stocks and bonds become increasingly a part of the daily lives of average citizens in industrialized countries, the profit motive increasingly permeates the politics of international capital distribution. Who, how, and what garners a portion of these ever-growing funds is decided by rate of return and this profit criteria goes increasingly unchallenged by a vested populace. The following chapters explore the political implications of this new system of capital distribution.

2
Institutional Investors as Political Actors

The 1994 Mexican peso devaluation and the 1997 Asian Crisis emphasized the power international financial globalization can have in developing countries. Many scholars as well as more mainstream 'experts' on financial globalization refer to this new power using abstract concepts such as the 'market' and 'financial integration'. Scholars in economics and international political economy often refer to the phenomenon of 'integration' to describe the global processes that have increasingly inter-mingled emerging markets with the more mature, developed financial markets. (Garrett, 1998; Frieden, 1999) This 'integration' is often seen as the primary force behind emerging market successes and failures.[1] Other scholars, such as Kingstone (1999), Stone (1999), and Unger (1999), refer to this power as 'the market' or 'market forces'. Kingstone and Stone, for instance, see the 'market' as the enforcer of monetary and fiscal discipline for Brazil and Russia, respectively.[2] More popularly, Thomas Friedman, *Wall Street Journal* columnist and author, describes this power as the 'herd' in his *New York Times* best-selling book, *The Lexus and the Olive Tree* (1999). Friedman emphasizes that the financial herd, or 'short-horn cattle,' is bigger and more diverse than ever before. He defines the herd as 'millions of investors moving money around the world with the click of a mouse' (Friedman 1999: 11). In an imagined response to Malaysian Prime Minister Dr. Mahathir Mohamad's September 1997 denouncement of George Soros and other financiers for the crash in the ringitt, for instance, Friedman predicts Robert Rubin would have said:

> And the most basic truth is this: *No one is in charge* – not George Soros, not 'Great Powers' and not I.... You keep looking for someone to complain to, someone to take the heat off your markets, someone to blame. Well, guess what, Mahathir, there's no one on the other end of the phone. I know that's hard to accept. It's like telling people there's no God. But the global marketplace today is an Electronic Herd of often anonymous stock, bond, currency and multinational investors, connected by screens and networks (Friedman, 1999: 93–4).

In essence, Friedman contends that, unlike previous decades, today's financial markets contain so many investors that individual firms can longer be held accountable for the movements of the 'market' in developing countries. In some ways, this is the case. With an increase of 401K holdings and 43 per cent of US households holding some form of stock, it appears that the democratization of finance has begun (Weisbrot, 1999: 3). However, upon closer observation, this pluralism that appears to diffuse the power of large investors, is not as amorphous as Frieden and others speculate. The average household has only US$14,000 in the market and the top 10 per cent of households have received 86 per cent of the stock market gains since 1989 (Weisbrot, 1999: 3).

Echoing this conceptualization of the abstractness of the market through its apparent 'democratization' over a decade before, Jeffry Frieden quotes 'the most prominent spokesperson for the American international banking community' Walter Wriston, on his views of the global economy (1987: 114–15):

> The gold standard, replaced by the gold exchange standard, which was replaced by the Bretton Woods arrangements, has now been replaced by the information standard. ... The last thing the political process wants is to be accountable. But there's nothing the politicians can do. The information standard, the information-intensive society, moves accountability from a few knowledgeable men and women to the population. Internationally, it moves it to a judgment of the way your policies [a country's] look to the international markets.

Wriston and Friedman portray the international financial market as a nebulous reality that exerts a healthy discipline upon politicians in developing countries. Leslie Elliott Armijo has done some of the most comprehensive work on private capital flows' impact on the politics of developing countries (Armijo, 1999). Armijo provides a framework for analysing the possible political consequences of the different types of capital inflows into developing countries (Armijo, 1999). Although Armijo suggests that it is nearly impossible to link directly foreign capital inflows and democratization, she presents a three-stage argument that hypothesizes the potential connections between the two. In the first stage, she divides capital inflows into six categories and suggests the probable domestic beneficiaries of each. In the second stage, Armijo theorizes the potential impact of these capital inflows on four intermediate variables, economic growth, political resources, financial crises and pressure for neo-liberal policies. One of the premises of this argument is that different types of capital inflows strengthen different domestic political actors. Hence, capital inflows impact democratization through the strengthening of the domestic recipient. Foreign capital will either increase or decrease the power of domestic political actors. For example, if foreign capital flows to a government, the power of the incumbent, either authoritarian or democratic, is increased. If flows go to local businesses, political contestation can increase but not necessarily participation. Thus it is possible that the power of the business community is increased, but it is not a given.

In addition to her theory of the importance of who is receiving the capital flows, Armijo considers some of the possible macroeconomic effects produced by the various types of capital inflows. For instance, she sees those types of foreign capital inflows that may have links to economic growth (foreign direct investment, and portfolio flows and long-term bank loans to local big businesses) as having potentially positive effects on democratization. However, on a macroeconomic level, portfolio flows run the risk of producing balance of payments crises, as well as fiscal crises, both of which can be disruptive to democratic consolidation. Furthermore, Armijo cites the possibility that institutional investor pressure for neo-liberal economic reform may force incumbent governments to choose policies that lead to the eventual inhibition of political democracy. In particular, Armijo suggests that the oft-assumed complementarity between a free market and democracy is false in the short and medium term, and that economic liberalization may actually hurt transitional democracies. Thus, according to Armijo, institutional investors may indirectly influence democracy in developing countries through their preferences for neo-liberal reform. However, the recipient of the capital and the associated macroeconomic conditions produced by this type of flow are the main influences on democratization according to Armijo.[3]

Understated in Armijo's work, and obscured by Stone, Kingstone, Friedman, and Wriston, is the level of coordination and potential power of institutional portfolio investors. Now controlling the majority of capital inflows, institutional investors' impact on the developing world cannot be underestimated. Without the organizational structures of the multilateral bureaucracies, the centrality of foreign policy, and the consistency of incremental budgeting, power over capital flows appears to be diffused, governed now by the intangible market mechanisms of supply and demand. In Armijo's analysis, democratic processes are most affected by capital inflows through the benefits that accrue to the recipients of these funds. Any systemic changes in the selection process of, and/or control over recipients, are compressed into this framework. However, this chapter suggests it is not only the laws of supply and demand that are impacting democratic processes but also the conventions and preferences of institutional investors. The following section is a two-tier argument establishing the possibility that institutional investors have the capability to be political actors in developing countries. First, emerging market fund managers are at the center of portfolio flows to developing countries and possess the power to influence market flows. Secondly, their investment decisions are not simply objective assessments of market value but are also the result of their own subjective environment as defined by their peers.

Are emerging markets 'efficient'?

This rise in portfolio equity investments to developing countries, and the probability of its continued increase, prompts the question, how are these funds from advanced industrialized countries allocated to the emerging markets? As the origins of capital inflows shift from public to private sources, one could expect a dissipation of distributional control as market mechanisms take the place of aid agencies. In determining the amount of control investors may have (in spite of market mechanisms), two key elements of the allocation system are the level of market inefficiencies and the degree to which funds are 'pushed' or 'pulled' into developing countries. In other words, to what extent is the allocation of funds governed by the market versus controlled by investors? First, if these funds were allocated in a completely fair and efficient market, in which information flows freely and there is equitable access, this would disallow an inordinate amount of control by any investor or groups of investors. Secondly, if the amount of private capital inflows into developing countries depended solely on factors exogenous to these countries, then distributional control would be non-existent as well and market mechanisms would prevail.

However, if, for example, investors show signs of grouping around a norm, or individual institutional investors are not making independent decisions, then this indicates a departure from a competitive and efficient market. I contend that the investment decisions of emerging market fund managers are not simply objective assessments of market value but are also the result of their own subjective environment as defined by their peers.

The premise held by free market advocates such as Friedrich Hayek and Milton Friedman, is that the best and fairest way to allocate goods is to allow the market to operate unimpeded by human intervention (Hayek, 1944; Friedman, 1962). If accompanied by proper laws allowing free access and fair competition, supply and demand will sort out inefficiencies. As more developing countries adopted the idea that market mechanisms are better suited to allocate resources than public enterprises, the focal point of development debates became how best to implement economic reforms that move toward this neo-liberal ideal. A large part of these economic reforms has been the development and implementation of a financial infrastructure grounded in this free market goal. In particular, emerging securities markets, a subset of this trend, have been the focal point of many liberalization efforts. However, the level of efficiency of these developing stock exchanges appears relatively weak, bringing into question the relative fairness of the market.

Efficiency, in capital markets, has two definitions. First, the operational definition refers to the relative competitiveness of brokers within the market. This can be measured by the transaction costs charged for services. These costs are observed most easily in the differences between 'bid and ask' prices of a particular investment.[4] The second definition concerns pricing efficiency. Strong-form efficiency means that prices will always reflect both private and public information pertinent to the valuation of a security. Semi-strong efficiency exists if all public information is immediately reflected in the price of a stock. When financial theorists refer to an 'efficient market,' they are most commonly using the second definition of pricing efficiency. The following discussion also refers to pricing efficiency in emerging markets.

Financial theorists, it has been said, fall into two camps; those that believe financial markets are efficient and those that don't. When in 1973 Burton Malkiel published his well-known book, *A Random Walk Down Wall Street*, he set into motion what is now commonly referred to as the Efficient Market Hypothesis (EMH), a strong-form version of the random walk hypothesis. The much-debated EMH suggests that within securities markets, information is disseminated and assimilated almost immediately, causing the price of the security to reflect and continually incorporate all available public and private information. The implications of this assumption are that any type of analyses, from stock charts to earnings estimates, are useless. In other words, 'a blindfolded chimpanzee throwing darts at the *Wall Street Journal* could pick a portfolio of stocks that would perform as well as those carefully selected by the highest priced security analyst' (Malkiel, 1982: 44).

Other theorists have offered various refinements to the random walk hypothesis (Grossman and Stiglitz, 1976; Mader and Hagin, 1976; Diamond and Verrecchia, 1981; Garber, 1990). These refinements have engendered more sophisticated versions of the original hypothesis which take into account certain anomalies, such as the tulip mania (Garber, 1991) in which investors bandwagon around certain investments with an intrinsic value that suggests greater caution. In addition, the presence of volatility in certain stocks has also been analysed (Mader and Hagin, 1976).[5]

Others, however, have refuted the notion that markets are efficient and offer evidence suggesting that the use of econometric, technical, and fundamental analyses can help detect undervalued stocks, cyclical pricing, and correlation between pricing and other factors.[6] Through the detection of such market anomalies, one can exploit market opportunities and theoretically do better than the chimpanzee. In fact, the market in emerging country securities displays many characteristics of inefficiency.[7]

This chapter suggests that international portfolio flows into the emerging markets do not fulfill two of the primary conditions necessary for an efficient market.[8] First, the EMH assumes there are a sufficient number of investors in the market to warrant competition and render it impossible for any one investor to manipulate the market. Secondly, in a fair and efficient market, investors have access to roughly the same information and react similarly and 'rationally' within the confines of profit-maximization. Neither of these assumptions describes the reality of contemporary emerging market investing.

In addition, if by an 'efficient market' we mean a market in which funds are allocated to investments offering the highest rate of return; then we must recognize that from the viewpoint of the advanced industrial country investor, investments in advanced industrial countries and in emerging markets are substitutes for one another. If the rate of return in the US goes up then, obviously, the *relative* rate of return in Mexico, if it remains unchanged, will fall. While such investor behavior may be 'rational' and even 'efficient,' it is so from the viewpoint of the *investor* but not necessarily from the perspective of the emerging market country (EMC). In fact, what financial analysts term 'push' factors, are very important among the factors determining net flows into EMCs.

The argument that the shift in financial flows, in particular the growth of portfolio capital, has an impact on political liberalization in developing countries, implies that certain economic and political conditions within a country will attract investments, or that 'pull' factors matter. Although 'pull' factors were once thought to be the main determinant of country choice, this assumption has been challenged recently by theorists claiming the predominance of 'push' factors, or factors external to a country which encourage an increase in portfolio flows regardless of internal changes. If push factors are the main determinants of portfolio inflows, then policy choices within developing countries should be less constrained and the argument for the ability of portfolio investors to effect political liberalization is weakened.

There are several reasons to believe that 'push' factors are the most prevalent determinant of portfolio flows to developing countries. For instance, source country regulations were found correlated with the amount of capital flowing to emerging markets.[9] A recent study indicating a correlation between US and Mexican long-term financial assets provides further evidence external factors may have a strong impact on emerging market capital inflows.[10] Another analysis finds a higher correlation between the prices of closed-end country funds and US equities, than the net asset value of individual foreign securities in the country funds.[11] In other words, emerging market country fund investments are related more to US market performance than emerging market stock valuation. In all of these cases, these 'push' advocates find little correlation between economic conditions in emerging market countries and the prices of emerging market stocks.[12]

In addition to the correlation found between external factors and emerging market investments, certain strategies for allocating equity investments to developing countries have led to the conclusion that developing countries can do little to influence the inflows into their countries. Portfolio allocations are chosen based on the risk tolerance and investment goals of the investor. Often, the first step in professional asset allocation is to decide how money will be divided between particular investment instruments. These decisions are usually made by the first level of money managers within a bank, pension fund or even at the individual level. Emerging market investments are considered foreign stock and fall into the category of a high-risk international investment. External factors such as the source country's interest rate expectations are taken into account during this first-level allocative phase of investor strategy. If the US market is bearish due to high interest rates for instance, emerging markets may present portfolio managers with international diversification and a high growth alternative. Professional portfolio investors most frequently decide which portion of their portfolio to allocate to the investment category of 'emerging markets' based on predetermined formulas for international diversification and the performance of the domestic markets in developed economies. Thus, a portfolio strategy is developed in which the percent of foreign-held equity is established before decisions are made about specific country allocations. For instance, one study suggests that a portfolio with less than 20 per cent invested in the Emerging Markets index is sub-optimal (Hartmann and Khambata, 1993: 100).[13] As defenders of the 'push' thesis suggest, this percentage can change depending on factors exogenous to the appeal of specific emerging market countries, thus affecting the overall amount invested in the emerging markets.

Although 'push' factors probably determine the size of the pie, 'pull' factors presumably determine how it will be sliced. 'Pull' factors such as economic reform and political stability are the elements through which developing country governments can impact capital inflows. Here, the specialized role of the emerging market mutual fund manager becomes crucial. These experts rate the conditions that attract investment within developing countries, or the 'pull' factors, such as their gross domestic product (GDP) or economic policy. Through the management of pull factors, emerging market governments can attract the capital controlled by emerging market fund managers. The next part examines the potential capability of emerging market fund managers to influence the policies that shape a developing country's investment pull.

Behind the bulk of portfolio equity investments and bond purchases, and now a fair amount of FDI, are institutional investors: the money managers of mutual funds, pension funds, insurance companies, banks, brokerage firms, and large multinational corporations. Estimates indicate that as much as 90 per cent of portfolio assets invested in emerging market equities involve institutional investors and the capital flowing to these investors continues to increase (Howell, 1995: 78). Mutual funds, managed by the large brokerage firms, increased their contribution to the emerging markets from US$6 billion in 1988 to US$81.5 billion in 1993 (IMF, 1995). Similarly, pension fund contributions to the emerging markets have risen from just US$500 million in 1990 to US$18 billion in 1993 (Lee, 1995). A research team predicts that pension funds will continue to invest larger and larger amounts in the emerging markets, with the period between 1995 and 2000 expected to be one of the highest rates of growth. A survey shows that pension funds are expected to increase their international holdings from 3.5 per cent in 1990 to 12.2 per cent in 1999.[14]

Most institutions, i.e. pension funds, insurance companies, and banks, however, do not control their individual investments into emerging markets. Due to the high cost of travel, data collection, and transaction fees, it is frequently more cost-effective to use specialists within the field of emerging markets to choose the countries and sectors in which to invest. This is even more the case when smaller investors want to invest in emerging markets. Barings Securities reported US mutual funds alone constituted 62 per cent of all net inflows to emerging market equities in 1993 (Malas, 1995: 23).[15] The cost-effectiveness and benefits of specialization, combined with the great increase in portfolio flows to emerging markets, has created a group of individuals with enormous power over private resource flows to developing countries, namely, emerging market mutual fund managers.

In her thesis, Armijo cited the possibility that institutional investor pressure for neo-liberal economic reform may force incumbent governments to choose policies that could be problematic for political democracy. However, as previously stated, Armijo understates the role of institutional investors and underestimates the impact international financiers may have on democratization. The remainder of this chapter will highlight the importance of the individuals behind these market processes.

Emerging markets mutual fund managers and concentration of power

Estimates indicate that emerging market fund managers may control as much as 55 per cent of portfolio flows to emerging markets.[16] In the month of January 1996, over US$1 billion was put into emerging market equity funds (Prochniak, 1996). The reason for this enormous amount of control may lie with the cost-effectiveness of specialization. Foreign investing costs the typical institutional investor much more than domestic investing. The high cost of maintaining in-country analysts, navigating a foreign financial infrastructure and paying transaction fees; has made the services of emerging market specialists very attractive to the average institutional investor.

One way to examine the decision rules that govern the channeling of money into emerging market mutual fund managers is to examine the portfolio holdings of the largest emerging markets funds – Templeton Developing Markets. Mark Mobius, manager of the various Templeton emerging market funds, commands a mammoth presence in the emerging markets arena. Referred to as 'the reigning king of emerging-market funds' and an 'emerging markets guru', Mobius was responsible for over US$10 billion of emerging market fund assets in 1998 (Mellow, 1998). To illustrate how institutional money is funneled into the hands of one fund manager, the institutional holdings within one of Mobius' funds are listed (see Table 2.1). These holdings, comprised mostly of banking and other securities-related firms, give a preliminary indication of the reliance of other institutional investors on such specialists as Mobius.

The presence of investors as large as Barclays, Chase Manhattan, and Bear Stearns within Mobius' portfolio, challenges Friedman's notion that, the [equity] market is made up of 'a million investors moving money around with the click of a mouse' (Friedman, 1999: 11).[17]

Another dimension of the concentration of power appears when one examines the clumping of assets within one of the main vehicles for emerging market investors: the emerging market mutual fund. In its 1997 database, Reuters lists only 56 funds that fall into the category of emerging market funds in the US and Europe.[18] The

Table 2.1 Institutional investors' holdings of templeton developing markets

Investor	Industry	Shares held
Alex Brown & Ass.	Securities	7,178
American National Bank & Trust	Banking	2,036
Bank One Investment	Investment bank	11,892
Barkclays Bank	Banking	173,226
Baring Private Investment Trust	Securities	747,632
Bear Stearns & Co.	Securities	12,639
Chase Manhattan	Banking	42,000
Chicago Trust Co.	Banking	67,000
A.G. Edward & Sons	Securities	10,271
Franklin Resources	Securities	110,300
Mercury Asset Mgt	Unit trust	982,008
Norwich Union	Banking	979,335
Smith & Williams Growth Trust	Unit trust	198,915
Treadneedle Investment	Offshore fund	850,000
Valley Forge Asset Mgt	Securities	168,080

*Second quarter filings, 1996.

Source: Bloomberg Data Files, June 1996.

Table 2.2 Concentration of emerging markets funds, second quarter, 1996*

Management group	% of assets of top 50 funds
Templeton	32
Fidelity	13
Morgan Stanley	13
Montgomery	9
Merrill Lynch	5
Total	72

*Top 50 emerging market funds, excluding regional and specific funds, but including both equity and income funds.

Source: Reuters Money Network Research Data on CD-ROM, June 1996.

top 50 of these emerging market funds total over US$13 billion in assets.[19] Within this fund universe, five institutional investors hold 72 per cent of these assets. The Templeton fund alone held a 32 per cent share of these funds (see Table 2.2). In addition to the concentration of assets found in this geographical mandate, regional funds also show similar characteristics. According to Trustnet, an investment advisory service disseminating information on international mutual funds, of the 26 emerging Asia funds listed, three institutions control 59.7 per cent of assets totaling over US$9 billion. Similarly, three institutions control 59.3 per cent of the assets in 19 Latin American regional funds.[20]

Such funds wield considerable influence. Evidence of the power of these firms is apparent when one of them comments positively or negatively about a particular country and that country's stock exchange reacts. Merrill Lynch, with the lowest portion of assets held among these five, has demonstrated its ability to sway the markets with the weight of its investments. In May 1996, the International Finance Corporation's *Monthly Review of Emerging Markets* reported that both the Chilean and Colombian markets were affected by the actions of one investor. In early May 1996, Merrill Lynch recommended that investors reduce their holdings in Chile and, according to the IFC's emerging market database, 'equities lost ground ... following [this announcement]' (IFC, May 1996: 18). In addition, Colombia's stock market responded favorably when Merrill Lynch raised its recommended allocation for investment in Colombia

(IFC, May 1996: 22). Furthermore, when global equity strategist for Morgan Stanley, Barton Biggs, announced in 1993 that he was 'maximum bullish' on China, the Hong Kong stock exchange, which holds a great portion of Chinese stocks, shot up considerably (Shameen, 1996: 1). Biggs was also responsible for the leap in Toyko's stock market in November 1998. The Wall Street Journal reported that the Nikkei, the Toyko stock exchange, increased 575 points, or 4.1 per cent; and foreigner buyers traded 17 million more buy orders than sell because of a couple of statements made by Biggs. Biggs commented that 'Japan could be the next great trade' and increased his recommended allocation of Japanese stocks in a model world portfolio. This was the biggest increase in the Nikkei in the last two months. These examples highlight the amount of power wielded by the top emerging market strategists.

Coordination and emerging market fund managers

In addition to the concentration of power and assets within a few emerging market funds, evidence exists to suggest that the decisions of these fund managers are coordinated. The following analysis tests for coordination between institutional investors, with coordination defined as a correlation of action, intentional or not, occurring between groups of investors. To test whether or not institutional investors could function coherently as political actors in developing countries, it is necessary to show that in making their investment decisions they are not simply reacting independently to the same macroeconomic and risk statistics, but are influenced by principles, norms and/or information exchanges between investors. If this were the case, then developing countries' economic and political destinies are not solely subject to the dictates of an invisible hand but are also in the hands of institutional investors.

The test for coordination between investors assumes that, if fund managers from a certain geographic area systematically coordinate their decisions with one another (but systematically differ from fund managers located elsewhere), then one has uncovered *prima facie* evidence of non-market coordination. In other words, if investors do not coordinate and allocate simply according to macroeconomic and risk data, then factors exogenous to emerging countries' economic and political rating should not matter. For instance, if investors frequent the same associations or share information on the trading floor then this would indicate one level of coordination, and a violation of the EMH. If the EMH worked, then each country should be receiving approximately the same allocations from fund managers whose investment objectives and regional mandates are the same. At the very least, correlation between funds in the US should not be any greater than correlation of funds without regard to location.

First, the geographic allocations of 18 emerging market funds, 8 US-based and 10 European, using 1996 second quarter reports were compared. All funds based in the US are traded on the New York exchange, and 8 of the 10 European funds are traded on the London exchange. These funds, all under the investment category of 'emerging market' growth funds, are equity funds with the same investment objectives.[21] Two types of analysis are performed on these funds to determine what effect, if any, fund location may have on the percentage a fund allocates to a particular country. The third analysis looks at two fund locations that are even farther apart, Japan and the US and compares emerging market stock holdings of Japanese and American investors at the end of 1995.

Testing for coordination

In order to test for coordination in general, a universe of emerging market funds was chosen from the same period and with the same investment objectives. The funds chosen were all explicitly emerging market funds, meaning that at least 80 per cent of their holdings were invested in emerging market countries. In addition, visibility of the fund and availability of information were criteria. Not all funds made available their holdings for this period and funds that were relatively obscure were excluded. Funds that focused on a particular region, such as an East Asian fund or a Bangladesh fund, were also excluded.

Two tests were then performed to see if fund location influenced country allocation. The first test was simply a comparison of the mean allocations per country by location. For instance, if country A received a greater average allocation from US-based funds, this would indicate that the location of the fund might impact the portfolio choices of the managers. A comparison of means illustrates the overall portfolio allocations of US- and European-based funds. By forming an average country allocation for each group of funds, a portfolio was constructed to show the differences in mean distributions. The results are reported in both chart and table formats and serve to give the reader a visual reference for comparison. The second test compared the average correlation between fund locations. Correlation on geographic distribution between all funds should approximately equal correlation between funds traded in New York and funds traded outside of New York. This test for comparing average correlation was constructed by forming three correlation matrices, a European–European, US–US, and a European–US fund matrix. The average correlation between funds was then calculated for these matrices. If the average correlation among US or among European funds were greater than the average correlation between European and US funds, this would indicate a level of coordination based on fund location. A full matrix of all the funds is included.

Results

The comparison of means resulted in significant differences in fund allocation based on location. There were considerable differences between fund allocations to certain countries, particularly those of the larger emerging market countries: Brazil, Hong Kong, Malaysia, Mexico and Thailand. These variances and the differences in the smaller emerging market countries are highlighted in Table 2.3. The results of the most striking differences between European and US funds are also represented there.

Table 2.3 Differences in country allocations by location of emerging market fund

European-based funds		NY-based funds	
% more than NY funds		% more than European funds	
Korea	186	Greece	100
Russia	107	Portugal	100
India	100	Taiwan	100
Peru	100	Venezuela	100
Singapore	100	Mexico	87
Thailand	68	Brazil	75
Indonesia	61	Poland	56
China	31	Hong Kong	43
Malaysia	27	Philippines	30

Source: Second quarter reports, 1996.

The less noticeable differences are between the smaller emerging market countries and these are also highlighted in Table 2.3. Table 2.3 highlights some of the larger differences between US and European institutional investors' geographic distribution choices for emerging market mutual fund portfolios. Several findings signify the possible influence of fund location on fund country distributions. First, US investors seem to have shied away from investments in India, Singapore and Peru entirely during this period. Of the funds included in this analysis, no US fund reported any of these three countries in their top ten holdings. Possible explanations are that European funds, primarily based in London, have many more historical ties to India and Singapore. Peru, a much smaller market, may be an anomaly, or possible low US investment here has been due to its status as a pariah among US investors due to the large amount of 1970's debt overhang. In the latter half of 1996, Peru picked up significantly in US holdings because of the success of debt restructuring through Brady bond issues. Conversely, European-based funds show no top-ten holdings for Greece, Portugal, Taiwan, and Venezuela but allocated larger portions of their portfolios to Malaysia, China, Indonesia, and Thailand.[22] Another important difference reveals US investors' significantly larger allocations to Brazil and Mexico and their significantly smaller distributions to Korea and Russia. During the quarter reported, European funds invested over 100 per cent more in Korean and Russian equities than their American counterparts. US fund managers preferred Mexico and Brazil, investing 87 per cent and 74 per cent more respectively than European managers. That US funds would prefer the larger Latin American countries to Southeast Asia is not surprising given the historical and geographical ties between the Americas. It is also not surprising that European funds, primarily out of London, would gravitate to Southeast Asia given their colonial history there. Although preliminary, these differences emphasize the possibility that a manager's subjectivity may influence country allocation and that market mechanisms are not the only determinant of emerging market equity flows.

The results of comparing the correlation between funds within the US and between funds in Europe indicate that there is a much higher correlation within US funds than between US and European funds. The average correlation within US funds was 0.54 while the average correlation between US and European funds was only 0.18. The average correlation within funds based in Europe was 0.36, much lower than US funds. One of the apparent reasons for this is that not all the funds are traded on the same exchange. One of the funds, Crédit Lyonnais Emerging Market Fund, is traded on the Singapore exchange and its parent company is French. When Crédit Lyonnais is excluded, the average correlation for European funds increased (to 0.40). All other European funds are traded on the London exchange, indicating that correlation is higher around similar locations and that a shared exchange could be a factor.

A closer look at the correlation also shows that there is a much lower correlation between the Crédit Lyonnais and US funds. Unsurprisingly, this might suggest coordination between the London exchange and New York exchange is higher than between New York and Singapore, where Crédit Lyonnais is traded. The highest correlation between funds was between the Montgomery Emerging Markets Fund and the Montgomery Emerging Markets Institutional Fund, not surprising given the funds share a common manager. This suggests that fund managers based in the same corporation allocate across their funds in a similar manner. In other words, although a fund manager may manage different funds, the criteria used to determine country allocations are the same. This tendency also suggests that there is potentially little difference in geographic distributions between a fund specifically designed for institutional investors, Montgomery Emerging Markets Institutional Fund, and a fund for investors in general, Montgomery Emerging Markets Fund. The emerging market fund manager chooses country allocations in a similar manner for both.

Table 2.4 gives an idea of the level of correlation between US and European funds only.

As Tables 2.1–2.4 indicate, there is a much stronger correlation within US funds and within European funds than between them. This fact provides evidence that investors do coordinate. The location of the fund helps to determine the type of country allocations that will be made. The results also suggest that the closer the exchanges are, the stronger correlation may be.[23]

A quick look at Japan's foreign stock holdings provides additional evidence that the operations of the supposedly impersonal global marketplace remain rather more subjective and culture bound than

Table 2.4 Correlation matrix for European and US funds, June 1996 (US funds in italic)

	abtr	for	gov	gen	bari	cl	klei	murr	buch	flem	msem	trow	bea	temp	tcw	gt	mgm	mgmi
abtr																		
for	0.65																	
gov	0.45	0.51																
gen	0.4	0.33	0.31															
bari	0.51	0.59	0.46	0.32														
cl	0.35	0.21	0.05	−0.21	0.12													
klei	0.11	0.49	0.08	0.05	0.21	0.29												
murr	0.41	0.48	0.45	0.44	0.24	0.004	0.29											
buch	0.42	0.37	0.35	0.19	0.81	0.3	0.25	0.24										
flem	0.48	0.7	0.59	0.29	0.76	0.09	0.36	0.34	0.49									
msem	0.47	0.5	0.61	0.25	0.52	0.21	−0.05	0.1	0.43	0.58								
trow	0.56	0.48	0.41	0.49	0.51	0.14	−0.06	0.28	0.35	0.48	0.61							
bea	0.42	0.52	0.55	0.76	0.43	−0.01	0.12	0.47	0.14	0.34	0.46	0.65						
temp	0.21	0.33	0.71	0.33	0.13	0.12	0.02	0.29	0.03	0.27	0.59	0.37	0.55					
tcw	0.55	0.65	0.8	0.43	0.65	0.04	0.34	0.58	0.64	0.7	0.37	0.49	0.46	0.44				
gt	0.1	0.34	0.64	0.2	0.27	−0.03	0.007	0.31	0.07	0.34	0.49	0.38	0.56	0.72	0.4			
mgm	0.66	0.73	0.63	0.35	0.77	0.25	0.33	0.42	0.67	0.86	0.63	0.72	0.44	0.32	0.83	0.34		
mgmi	0.71	0.79	0.62	0.41	0.71	0.22	0.28	0.57	0.58	0.77	0.59	0.71	0.52	0.35	0.8	0.36	0.94	

Note: See Appendix 1 for key to fund abbreviations.

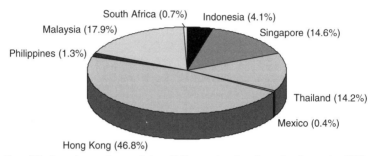

Figure 2.1   Japan's emerging market portfolio country allocations, fourth quarter, 1995
Source: Figures provided by Kazu Kijima of Shoken Toshintaku Kyokai of Tokyo, Japan.

is often recognized. Supporting the theory that fund location is a determinant in a fund's country allocation, a chart representing the Tokyo exchange's investments in emerging markets is presented. The portfolio breakdown here differs significantly from that of both the European and US funds.[24] Figure 2.1 indicates the differences in the geographic allocations of Japanese funds.

The heavy weighting of Japan's emerging market holdings in Hong Kong and Asia, and the lower rate of investment in Latin America, portray a significantly different geographic portfolio allocation than US and European funds. Again, fund location matters in the allocation of emerging market capital.

Conclusions

This chapter demonstrates that the fastest-growing sector of capital to developing countries is controlled by a small number of emerging market fund managers and that these investors coordinate. The location of the fund helps determine the type of country allocation that will be made. These two violations to the efficient market hypothesis, concentration of assets and coordination among investors, suggest that institutional investors, particularly emerging mutual fund managers, have accrued considerable power and invest according to factors external to information about investments. This coordination implies a degree of coherence and perhaps the existence of networks in which to form norms for investing, a prerequisite for expressing their preferences as a group. For instance, we know that the weight of one management firm can have the power to sway investments both to and away from, a country. This data also points to other dimensions of the emerging market investing that needs further exploration – the countries that get the majority of the portfolio flows are in Latin America, Asia, and Europe. No country in the Middle East, Central Asia or Africa made the top-ten list during this period. Furthermore, the results testing for coordination among these individuals suggest that there is a correlation between funds based on where the funds are managed, indicating investment choices are at least in part predicated on something other than independent information assessments. These findings indicate violations to the EMH, and support the contention that institutional investors, in this case emerging market mutual fund managers, coordinate. Chapters 3–5 will address around which issues investors coordinate, and how this coordination takes place.

3
Institutional Investor Preferences

If we agree that concentration and coordination exists among emerging market's institutional investors as discussed in prior chapters, then the preferences and actions of these institutional investors, as they influence the financial markets and politics in developing countries, are important to understand. In this chapter, institutional investors' devaluation of democracy and preference for stability is explored. In particular, this chapter scrutinizes some of the top emerging market fund managers' opinions about politics in developing countries. What emerges from a survey of various sources of information on emerging market investing is the finance community's indifference and occasional disdain for democracy as they voice their preferences for neo-liberal reform and stability over most other concerns.[1] This chapter will also discuss whether the preference for stability through authoritarianism might be correct in terms of its ability to achieve the economic results sought by investors. In other words, are investors wise to opt for stability at the possible cost of decreasing political liberalization?

Preferences of institutional investors: stability or democracy?

In his second inaugural address, Bill Clinton summed up his worldview of the partnership between democracy and the market by stating that now the world is 'where democracy and open markets are on the march together'.[2] The sentiment that believes democracy and markets go well together is echoed in the business press as well as it portrays democraticness as an important magnet for investors. For instance, *Business Week* reported in 1995 that India was more attractive to investors than other emerging markets because of its democratic traditions: 'At a time when Western investors are skittish about emerging markets, India still looks attractive. Unlike Mexico or China, it is a full-throated democracy that should make it more stable as it faces the challenges of reform' (Moshavi and Engardio, 1995: 48). Regarding emerging markets, in an address to New York investors in March of 1998, Jose Angel Gurria Trevino, Mexico's Minister of Finance, extolled the economic benefits of democracy as he states:

> The consolidation of democracy in Mexico based on citizen participation and a multi-party political system, is an element that clearly strengthens our economy. The independent agency in charge of the electoral process, the new public financing scheme for campaigns, and the granting of equal media access to political parties, are clear examples of Mexico's solid political institutions. The plurality in the Mexican Congress after the mid-term elections of July 6, 1997, are a concrete manifestation of our 'democratic normality,' as President Zedillo calls it (Gurria, 1998: 4).

He concludes his speech by stating, 'more democracy and stronger institutions are the necessary complement to sound economic policy' (Gurria, 1998: 4). Both business press and reports by emerging market government officials speak of democracy's attractiveness. In addition, scholars have contributed theories that suggest democracy is in fact more likely to spur growth, thus attracting investments, than less democratic states.[3] What is perhaps clearest among these various opinions is that capital has most frequently followed those countries with the highest likelihood of long-term stability and that well-established democracies usually can deliver this better than fledglings or more authoritarian states. However, with the weakening of traditional means of financing and official development assistance – both which tended towards a longer-term approach – plus the strengthening of the more mobile portfolio flows, the time horizons of capital and thus the preferences of those investing the capital have changed. The attractive promise of long-term stability appears to have been replaced by the allure of short-term stability in the midst of unpopular and quickly implemented economic reforms. In a survey of some of the main participants in this 'march', specifically international institutional investors, a different picture emerges. The preferences of emerging market institutional investors suggest that democracy is not a primary concern. In fact, stability and a consistently investor-friendly financial infrastructure are two of the primary criteria investors seek when investing in emerging markets, often at the expense of political democracy. How emerging market fund managers decide on where to invest can be a complex process. Once the decision is reached to allocate to the emerging markets, the 'push', the 'pull' factors are assessed and can be divided into two categories; micro- and macroanalysis. Microanalysis, or the bottom-up approach, focuses on company and industry statistics. It would typically include such indicators as the price-to-earnings ratio and corporate management. Macroanalysis, or the top-down approach, surveys macroeconomic and political risk factors of countries and determines investment allocations accordingly. Most emerging market funds utilize both approaches in varying degrees and directions. Which macro-factors dissuade or persuade investment, however, become the main determinants of country choice.[4] Furthermore, in the wake of the 1997 Asian Crisis, one analyst suggested 'the market is more discriminating with respect to differentials between emerging market sovereigns [debt issues]; highlighting the importance of country allocations as opposed to a homogenous view of emerging markets as a whole' (Cembalest, 1998: 4). In other words, the top-down approach is viewed as gaining in importance *vis-à-vis* the bottoms-up after the Asian Crisis. In the following sources, the two factors emphasized the most are, not surprisingly, economic growth and political stability.

The preferences of emerging market investors can be discerned from a variety of sources. Two of the most prominent of these sources are investor advisory publications for emerging markets and direct statements from emerging market fund managers. The examples that follow, though anecdotal, are cumulatively quite revealing.

In *The Handbook of Emerging Markets*, Robert Lloyd George cites several 'requirements needed for a successful emerging market' (George, 1993: 13). In descending order, the first three of these are political stability, sound currency, and low inflation. The next seven elements focus on legal, accounting and transparency issues for foreign investors. George goes on to encourage over-weighting Asia because of its population size 'coupled with other factors such as political stability and low inflation'. He recommends diversifying among the Asian markets to obtain what he sees as the two most important factors, growth and stability.

In addition to George's emphasis on growth and stability, he highlights the advantages of privatization to international investors by listing three of its achievements. The first, the reduction of government deficit, falls perhaps primarily into the category of economic reform. The second and third advantages, however, have greater immediate consequences for political democracy. The second, the creation of first-time shareholders, is important to George because this new class will 'tend to vote for pro-business and conservative policies'. The third advantage is that privatization 'diminishes the power of trade unions' (George 1993: 17). In these last two advantages, George states the perhaps obvious investor preference for political conservatism over worker rights.

Another publication, *New World Business*, offers investors an analysis of what makes an emerging market successful. Published by Euromoney Publications and Worldlink, and in association with several large banks, this edited volume begins its overview of emerging markets with a comparison between governmental choices of reform. Comparing shock therapy to gradual reform, Fiona Jebb writes that countries which get economic reform wrong must 'beware the ballot box' (Jebb, 1995: 8). Jebb cites the cases of Poland's ousting of right-wing Hanna Suchocka, the uprising in Chiapas, and the rise of Russian nationalist Vladimir Zhirinovsky, as examples of the political peril which can plague incumbent governments facing electoral challenges following the implementation of rapid and deep reforms. She then applauds the successes of China's gradual reform measures and emphasis on economic, not political reform. Although she fails to mention that China's record of political rights and civil liberties are in a different category than newly democratized nations, she does question whether 'democracy is a help or a hindrance to economic reform processes' (Jebb, 1995: 10).

Another source of advice to investors interested in the emerging markets is the academic business journals such as the *Columbia Journal of World Business*. In an issue devoted solely to the emerging markets phenomenon, Mark Hartmann and Dara Khambata list three categories of risk/return determinants in the emerging markets; changes in economic policy, external factors, and political risk. The first category highlights the importance of a government's ability to implement long-term economic reform and the liberalization of foreign portfolio investment, and suggests that 'the timing and extent of the effects of structural reforms on share prices depends on the faith that investors have in the government's ability to carry out the reforms' (Hartmann and Khambata, 1993: 92). Nigeria's inability to implement quickly its Structural Adjustment Program is cited as a reason for a 56 per cent decline in its equity markets in 1986 (Hartmann and Khambata, 1993: 92). However, 'once these reforms had been successfully implemented, the stock market rose, ending the year with a 40.9 per cent return (Hartmann and Khambata, 1993: 92). What Hartmann and Khambata fail to mention is the manner in which many of these reforms were implemented. Under the military rule of Ibrahim Babangida at the time, there was mounting domestic opposition to the reforms, accompanied by increased pressure from the international financial institutions. In order to implement reforms the regime 'resorted to repression... [and] the human rights cloak worn by the regime at its inception in 1985 became increasingly ill-fitting' (Herbst and Olukoshi, 1994: 494).

The second category listed in the article, external factors, is analogous to 'push' factors, which are, for the most part, beyond the control of the recipient country. The third category, political risk, is given equal weight with economic reform and external factors. Hartmann and Khambata begin the section on political risk with the statement that the 'long-term nature of equity investment implies a necessity for political stability' (1993: 93). Increased uncertainty over political future is cited as a reason for increased volatility in the emerging markets. Two of the most important determinants in choosing a country in which to invest, according to Hartmann and Khambata, are speed of economic reform and political stability.[5]

The newsletter *South Africa Investor* captured institutional investor indifference to political progress in a survey conducted by the Investor Responsibility Research Center in January 1995. Included in the survey were 68 institutional investment managers of pension funds, endowments, and investment banks.[6] Although the survey revealed that 32 per cent were currently investing in South Africa and another 38 per cent were planning to in the future, the results do not support the hopes of many that investment is following the abolishment of apartheid. On the contrary, 'not a single respondent cited an investment vehicle that targets socioeconomic and infra-structural development as a top investment priority, and several respondents emphasized that investment return is the highest prior-ity for any investment they undertake in South Africa' (*South Africa Investor*, 1995: 10). Although it is unclear from the survey where sta-bility ranks *vis-à-vis* democracy, the results indicate investors did not respond positively to democratic transitions in South Africa.

The emphasis on the importance of stability in emerging markets can be found in the business press. After first commending the eco-nomic reforms in Mexico, in particular deregulation and privatiza-tion, *Business Week* then goes on to state: 'Then reality struck. Politics, ignored by money managers, overwhelmed economic con-siderations in Mexico…' (9 November 1995: 138). The advice then offered to investors was as follows:

Some of the best prospects for healthy earnings are in emerging markets. But the risk/reward ratio remains higher in Latin America and Asia, and money managers should recognize this cold, hard, fact. Money managers taking a second shot at higher returns in emerging markets would be wise to hire a few political risk ana-lysts, a couple of area specialists, and even one or two people who know something about military affairs. Political stability is as important as economic opportunity when investing in societies striving to make the difficult transition to capitalism and democ-racy (*Business Week*, 1995: 138).

The advice to hire political risk analysts is based on the assump-tion that money managers, focusing too much on economic statis-tics, may overlook the crucial component of political stability. This particular author even suggests that familiarity with military affairs may come in handy for investors, presumably as it relates to the sought-after stability.

Political risk analysts also highlight the importance of political stability as they offer assessments on individual countries. A sample report on Vietnam obtained from Political Risk Services via the Internet demonstrates this point. In mapping out the risk factor for potential investors, Political Risk Services forecasts the likelihood of turmoil based on which regime is most likely to be in power. An 18-month turmoil forecast suggests that if the Communist Party of Vietnam, or CPV, remains in power, then the turmoil factor should remain at the same low level.

In this scenario, the forecasts predicts that the military and security forces 'will enthusiastically follow any orders to repress dissidents... and [the] government will also move quickly to protect foreign firms if any turmoil threatens' (10 January 1995). If, on the other hand, the more liberal faction of the CPV were to gain power, the analysts foresee more potential for disruptions. In particular they cite the probability that 'labor would feel free to strike for higher wages' and the government, 'reluctant to use harsh, repressive tactics' would more likely be unsupported by the military and security forces. The third scenario possible, that the CPV hard-liners would come to power, would bring an initial rise in turmoil but 'the regime would employ the internal security forces and even the military to suppress opposition and restore order. Turmoil would then quickly return to its current low level. Foreign firms would be safe from turmoil after this government was firmly established...' (Political Risk Services, 1995). Essentially, this political risk analysis suggests that the best scenarios for investors are the ones in which either the moderates or hard-liners are in power, thus maintaining control over labor, wages, and other potential disruptions to the existing order of things. The most dangerous scenario would be if the liberal faction of the CPV came into power and started opening the door to what the analysts refer to as 'turmoil'. This turmoil, however, containing the freedom for labor to strike and the freedom from a government willing to repress demonstrations, begins to look like a move towards a more democratic regime. Apparently, as these political analysts suggest, the absence of this type of 'turmoil' is what investors seek.

Another venue for observing some of the top emerging market manager preferences is through direct statements by these investors. Clinton's aforementioned statement represents the traditional neoliberal belief that democratization and the opening of markets are natural partners. A common assumption has been that once a country adopts a constitution and holds elections, foreign investment will follow. However, in sharp contrast to this belief, Mark Mobius suggests that democracy is not a necessary condition when deciding where to invest. Instead, he recommends that investors look for good economic indicators and ignore the absence of democracy:

> Western-style democracies are not a requirement for prosperity and economic growth. Singapore is a case in point. In fact, Western-style democracies are generally unique in the developing world. In Asia, for example, functioning free wheeling democracies are the exception rather than the rule (Mobius, 1995: 122).

In addition to the advice Mobius gives in his book on emerging markets, he offers guidance to investors in prominent business publications. In an interview with *Fortune*, Mobius suggests that buying into a country when it is in turmoil may be the best strategy because other investors may be avoiding it for this reason. 'Buy when blood is running in the streets' he recommends.[7] Another anecdote is found in his advice to invest in Nigeria, despite its unrest stemming from a military takeover. '"Sure Nigeria is a mess" [Mobius] says cheerfully, "but we have a saying that by the time you see the light at the end of the tunnel, chances are it's too late"' (Cox, 1997). These statements indicate Mobius adheres to a well-known investor tenet, buy before others buy; and, in this case, before stability arrives and brings with it other investors. Here, Mobius also gives further indication of the yardstick by which countries are to be judged. The phrase 'blood running in the streets' suggests not simply callousness toward political unrest that has reached violent proportions, but also a confidence that the quelling of this unrest will attract further investment. The cavalier attitude implied by Mobius' Nigeria statement suggests that the usurpation of legitimate governance and the despotism that has plagued Nigeria in the 1990s, should perhaps be of little concern to foreign investors. Mobius admits that the politics of a country are of secondary concern and are relevant only in how they may 'impinge upon the profitability of the company' (Spragins and McGinn, 1995: 52).

As a reason to invest, politicians and business media often cite democracy in developing countries. However, as the above citations indicate, democracy's attractiveness among institutional investors is questionable. Another example of a leading investor's attitude towards democracy, is expressed by Rimmer de Vries, Senior Vice President and

Chief Economist for Morgan Guaranty Trust, as he warns prospective investors of the dangers of democracy:

> Two additional deterrents to foreign…investment have arisen in recent years in heavily indebted LDC's. One is heightened uncertainty associated with transition to more representative forms of government, whether in Latin America or the Philippines. The new democracies have sought to revise laws and practices put into place by dictatorial regimes in the 1960s and 1970s and, in so doing, have opened protracted debates of private property rights and the participation of foreign capital (de Vries, 1990: 97).

In particular, de Vries cites Brazil as the 'most lamentable case' because of the drafting of its new constitution which has 'greatly upset the business climate' (de Vries, 1990: 97). He suggests that the new constitution is an obstacle to foreign direct investment because it will seek to limit foreign direct investment that is not in the national interest. He is further discouraged by the inclusion of text that limits prospecting for 'strategic materials' to Brazilian companies.[8]

In contrast to his dislike of Brazil at this time, de Vries cites the counter example of Chile in the 1970s and early 1980s as a country making all the right decisions to enhance their investment potential. He lauds Chile's successes accomplished during the military rule of Pinochet, in particular, the increases in the efficiency of government-owned enterprises and the sweeping privatization programs of the 1980s. Although faced with difficulty in servicing its foreign debts, de Vries praises Chile for sticking to a liberal, export-oriented, foreign trade and payments regime. Not surprisingly, Chile increased its inflow of FDIs from US$70 million in 1983 to over US$1 billion in 1988 (Wallace, 1990: 100).

As of 1990, de Vries saw Chile as the only debt-burdened LDC to improve radically its business climate with deregulation and privatization. The only mention of the means to accomplish this politically, i.e. through a military dictatorship, is made when de Vries admits that Chile's 'favorable business climate could yet be affected by the coming transition from a dictatorial to a democratic regime' (de Vries, 1990: 100).

Another prominent name in emerging markets is Antoine van Agtmael. Agtmael spent eight years at the International Finance

Corporation and left in 1987 to establish the Emerging Markets Investors Fund in Washington DC. Here, he and his 32 employees manage over US$2.8 billion worth of assets (Klebnikov, 1994: 145). A central part of his investment strategy is found in his statement 'We ignore politics, taxes and currencies' (Klebnikov, 1994: 146). In 1994 he openly states his preference for the more authoritarian countries of China, Morocco, Korea, and Peru while expressing his aversion to countries with more representative politics, like Brazil and India (Klebnikov, 1994: 146).

Another internationally known institutional investor, Barton Biggs, isn't shy about making his preferences known. Biggs, head of Morgan Stanley Asset Management and named by *Institutional Investment* magazine the top global equity strategist for 1996, is one of the most powerful voices on Wall Street. As one business journalist puts it, 'more often than not, markets world-wide respond once Biggs makes his recommendations' (Shameen, 1996: 1). In an interview with *Asia Week*, Biggs comments on the rationale for some of his portfolio picks and conveys his thoughts on the importance of some political factors in attracting investment. Responding to the question, 'how bullish are you on the rest of Asia?' Biggs says that he is very optimistic in spite of 'the Western media…now going through a burst of pessimism about Asia' (Shameen, 1996: 2). He states:

> People are starting to question the lack of democracy in Asia, the high level of corruption in some countries and the continuing ability of many Asian companies to translate economic growth into earning-per-share growth. This is a whole line of baloney. I think it's ridiculous to harp on about these and other worries… (Shameen, 1996: 2).

In mid-October 1997, Biggs joined other money managers to reduce holdings in Asian emerging markets due to currency fears. This exodus of large money managers helped precipitate the greatest plunge of Hong Kong's stock market in history, a drop of 14.6 per cent at one point. Biggs commenting on his reasons for withdrawal from the region told the *New York Times*:

> I went out there last week and saw first hand that it was a mess. …What really bothered me is that the governments of these

countries were not doing the tough things they have to do to clear the markets (Faison, 1997: D1).

Although not stating what is needed to fix the markets, Biggs presumably is referring to the lack of institutional arrangements that structure the market in industrialized countries. Biggs is more direct in stating his preferences for the more authoritarian forms of government in an interview that took place in the Bahamas at Morgan Stanley's 1996 annual meeting of the world's 50 top investors. Commenting on the reasons South Korea had done so poorly the last seven years, Biggs states:

> It's still doing badly, for a variety of reasons. One has to do with the fact that it's very helpful to have a dictatorship in the bootstrap stage of an emerging market and an emerging economy. Dictators make the tough decisions and demand the sacrifices that have to be made to turn a poor country into a wealthy one. But there is a price to be paid in terms of social disorder, which is usually very painful. And the price is paid not only in terms of the political system but also on the economic side. When wages have been held down for five or six years, they're going to soar 20% a year when the lid is lifted. That's what Korea has been going through (Armour and McGowan, 1996: 6).

The statement provides a unique window into the mindset of one of the most powerful international investors. It blatantly reveals the narrowness of his concerns. Looking solely at developing countries as markets for his capital, Biggs prefers dictators because, he believes, they can implement the austerity programs he and other investors deem appropriate. Biggs sees 'painful' problems, like 'social disorder' and 'wages rising,' arising from these dictatorships, yet fails to mention the pain the populace has endured in human rights abuses and short-term austerity measures that often enrich few and impoverish many. Presumably, when he talks of 'social disorder' he is not referring to the unjust social disruptions caused by a dictatorship, but to popular protests for democracy. Rising wages is seen as a price to be paid for the years of labor union repression and government regulations suppressing wages, both good things according to Biggs.

Commenting on other countries, Biggs believes that Malaysia is 'a first-rate country that's managed very well' (Armour and McGowan,

1996: 6). Malaysia, under authoritarian rule for decades, had attracted so many investors that, according to Biggs, was now too highly priced for investments. When asked about India, Biggs cited several positives, such as its size, the number of listed companies on its exchanges, its British accounting system, and the maturity of its stock market. However, he continues to say 'but it's a messy story because there is no conceivably worse form of government for a developing country than a coalition democracy without a majority ruling party' (Armour and McGowan, 1996: 7). Commenting on Indonesia, Biggs states 'there is going to be problems when President Suharto goes' (Armour and McGowan, 1996: 7). Indonesia's Suharto government, infamous for the atrocities it inflicted upon its population, appears to be a risky proposition without the promise of repression.

Biggs does not stand alone in his hopes that Suharto would stay in power. Shortly before Suharto stepped down from his post, CNBC aired a discussion of top institutional investors and their thoughts on the Indonesian protests against Suharto occurring at the time. David Malpass, Chief International Economist for a top institutional brokerage firm, speculating on the expectation that Indonesia's army would join student protests to overthrow Suharto, was doubtful of this and suggested that 'we shouldn't expect the worse' (Malpass, 1997). Two colleagues, Michael Hartnett of Merrill Lynch and Robert Hormats of Goldman Sachs, joined Malpass in his fear of Suharto's overthrow. Hormats noted how important the military had been in the past playing a 'stabilizing role', presumably to the benefit of investors. He voiced his fear that the 'military is now in factions' and how this could lead to problems for investors. Hartnett echoed their worries that the social unrest would spread and cause problems for investors.

After the protests succeeded in prompting Suharto's resignation and Indonesia made significant strides towards democracy with the election of Abdurrahman Wahid, investors maintained their concern with the dictator's absence. The *New York Times* captures this fear as it reports:

> The bankers, brokers and fund managers whom Indonesia's government must court to help pull the country out of its worst economic crisis in a generation expressed some doubts Tuesday whether the newly chosen president, Abdurrahman Wahid, and

his 35 cabinet ministers have the expertise and cohesion needed to become efficient crisis managers. Worse, they fear that the government, in its attempt to use unfamiliar democratic institutions to eradicate the corruption of its predecessor, may sacrifice economics in the name of popular justice (Arnold, 1999).

Within the same article, a currency strategist for JP Morgan represents this sentiment as he comments 'Democracy is a desirable form of government, but it's not necessarily the most efficient form of government' (Arnold, 1999). In the case of Indonesia, at least in the short term, investors appear suspicious of democracy and the transitions needed to achieve it.

Fund managers and investment firms also communicate their interpretations of politics in developing countries through their quarterly summaries to clients of past performances and country forecasts. Most often, these analysts reports suggest under-weighting or over-weighting a country within an emerging market portfolio based on their assessments of future economic performance, reform progress, and investor magnetism. Not surprisingly, evaluations of politics are filtered by the anticipated impact changing parties or regimes may have on economic progress and reform. However, many of these political assessments are quite revealing in their preferences. For instance, Smith Barney Inc. discusses Mexico's 1997 elections:

> The real impact of the election may not be apparent to investors until October, when the budget debate begins in the more democratic era. We believe labor will ask for a minimum wage hike equivalent to this year's inflation and that they will be less willing to roll over for the government, especially without Fidel Velasquez on the scene. We believe there is a decent potential for the budget battle to cool the equity outlook if prices have risen as we anticipate (Barrineau, 1997: 1).

In this statement, the impact of more democracy is especially worrisome because of its potential impact on the budget debate and the expansion of labor's political power. The increase of the minimum wage is an increasingly common concern among investors, as inflationary pressures cut into the real wages of emerging market workers.

In addition to these emerging market fund managers, other players in the emerging markets investment field have been explicit in their preference for stability. For instance, institutional investments in infrastructure financing depend on this 'stability' and expect recipient governments to offer assurances. Commenting on criteria for investments in infrastructure development projects, a fund manager of one of the largest insurance companies indicates his preference for stability, and the expectation of assurances from the recipient government:

> The operative word here is, of course, stable. Just how much stability is there in a private power project in an emerging country? Many lenders look to sovereign governments to ease their anxieties (Perry, 1994: 24).

and

> As individuals, lenders get paid to not lose the house money, and these projects carry great risk. Lenders need assurances and guarantees from the governments of the host countries. These financings can't just be user-fee driven – there just aren't that many institutions that are going to lend without guarantees (Perry, 1994: 24).

These statements indicate that the preference for stability extends beyond the emerging market fund manager.

The belief that authoritarian type governments are better for investors is echoed by such mainstream investment pundits as Harry Dent. Dent, famous for his research on the financial market implications of the baby boom generation, extends his demographic modeling to developing countries as well. His model shows a strong correlation between demographics and financial indicators and, as he claims, works best for industrialized countries with free markets. This is true, he believes, because in developing countries politics play such a vital role in determining economic welfare. This can distort the effectiveness of the model. For instance, the type of regime can make a big difference in determining financial market indicators. When asked if he believed authoritarian governments making good decisions were best for developing countries, he replied:

> Yes! Exactly. Look at China. They are totalitarian, top-down, even communist. They basically kill any free-marketer or revolutionary

and they are doing quite well. They have made many of the right decisions. Top-down management is best if the leaders make the right decisions.[9]

One hopes that the 'decisions' he refers to here are in the area of economics and not regarding the aforementioned killing. The implications for this type of attitude are important. First, using the language of business when referring to an authoritarian government as 'top-down management' is problematic in that it glosses over the absence of consent and freedom. Killing protesters is seemingly justified, or at the very least forgiven, by those focused on a country as an investment option. Secondly, valuing the ability of a government to implement 'the right decisions' implies that a particular set of decisions are the right ones, regardless of popular support. This assumption suggests that any policy decision with macroeconomic benefits, or more specifically, financial market benefits, is uniformly a 'right' decision. The level of civic participation in policy creation and implementation are treated as hindrances rather than indicators of policy correctness.

In a more publicized preference for stability over democracy, a Chase Manhattan-hired political scientist, working as an institutional investment consultant, outlined a set of prescriptions for the Zedillo government in January of 1995. Shortly after the December 1994 Mexican peso devaluation, Riordan Roett offered the following advice: Armed repression of the rebels of Chiapas, election-fixing, and stricter control over labor unions. Roett's letter to Chase clients provides a strong example of investor preference for stability over democracy.[10] Roett outlines three problems that the Zedillo government must address to keep the investment community happy. First, the problems in Chiapas must be addressed. Roett suggests that 'the [Mexican] government will need to eliminate the Zapatistas to demonstrate their effective control of the national territory and of security policy' (Roett, 1994; cited in Cockburn and Silverstein (1995: 3)). Secondly, Roett suggests that the upcoming state elections could undermine political stability and that 'the Zedillo administration will need to consider carefully whether or not to allow opposition victories if fairly won at the ballot box' (op. cit.). The third item of concern expressed by Chase executives and Roett is the threat that Zedillo may lose the traditional loyalty of the labor movement.

Even though Roett concedes that the 'fall in the value of the peso severely undercuts the capacity of the average Mexican worker to purchase the bare necessities of life', he worries that Zedillo might end up 'yielding to worker demands which [would] further aggravate the economic situation' (op. cit.). This letter was circulated not only between investors, but also among politicians in Washington DC and other members of the finance community.

Although many large investors appear to consistently value an authoritarian approach to implementing reform, not all investors have discounted the benefits of democratic rule. The investor most visibly vocal about his preference and advocacy for democracy has been George Soros. Soros, founder of the Soros Foundation, an organization committed to assisting countries achieve more open societies, appears to be something of an enigma to the investment community. After officially dropping out of the money business in 1992, Soros became a vocal commentator on global affairs. Although he made billions in the capitalist system, Soros has come out against capitalism because of its pernicious nature towards democracy. In his book entitled *The Crisis of Global Capitalism*, Soros conveys his belief that today's capitalism is a threat to open, democratic societies. This book and preceding articles in *Atlantic Monthly* and *Foreign Policy* introducing Soros' concern about the *laissez-faire* direction modern capitalism has taken, brought on scathing attacks by the investment community. *Fortune* ran an article by Rob Norton entitled 'George Soros: Billionaire, Genius, Fool' that attacked the *Atlantic Monthly* article by Soros entitled 'The Capitalist Threat'. In this article, Norton calls Soros' ideas 'a rodomontade of sloppy thinking' and he warns 'the danger of Soros' ranting is that it will win undeserved attention because of who he is'. Soros, Norton claims, is just unhappy with the countries 'that sprung up in the East since [1989], rife as they are with crime, confusion, and poverty' (Norton, 1997: 2). Soros, blaming some characteristics of modern capitalism for part of the East's problems, has simply not given these countries enough time. Norton rhetorically asks 'But could it be that…there's nothing wrong with capitalism?' (Norton, 1997: 2) In another attack, Rodiger Dornbush wrote in the *Financial Times* that Soros is 'not gifted with clarity of thought or a golden pen' and 'has no clue about what is done in financial economics research…' (Dornbush, 1998: 2). He calls Soros' conclusion 'a sanctimonious elaboration of the notion that markets undermine intrinsic values' (Dornbush, 1998: 2). Soros, to be sure, is an easy target. After making his billions through capitalism, he is now condemning the system that made him wealthy. However, Soros' defense of democracy at the expense of criticizing capitalism seems to have received the harshest criticism. The virulence behind these attacks perhaps reveals the underlying tenet that it is okay to preach about the virtues of democracy as long as it does not entail advocating a shift away from a free market system.

Are institutional investors right?

The preferences of these institutional investors do not necessarily coincide with much of the prevailing information available about the linkages between regime type and the relative success of implementing and maintaining successful economic reform. In fact, evidence from various scholars indicates that authoritarian regimes are perhaps no better than democratic regimes at improving economic performance through reforms (Remmer, 1986, 1990; Haggard *et al.*, 1990). This appears to be true for two primary reasons. First, authoritarian regimes do not appear any more likely to choose to implement unpopular reforms and secondly, relatively little evidence supports the implicit belief that the particular brand of reform advocated and required by investors will prove successful in achieving the desired results.

Institutional investors' preferences suggest that authoritarian regimes are more likely to choose and implement the economic reform strategies prescribed by investors and the IMF. However, little evidence exists that there is a significant difference between regime types in terms of the choice of economic reform strategies (Nelson, 1990). Remmer states: 'Authoritarian regimes may inspire greater outside investor confidence or otherwise surpass their democratic counterparts in economic management, but they are no more likely to initiate stabilization programs or to survive their political reverberations' (1986: 20). Bresser Pereira cautions that Remmer's conclusion must be modified by the contextual components of a democratic regime's likelihood to implement unpopular reforms. He notes that 'when populist leaders in Argentina, Bolivia, Venezuela, Peru, and Brazil adopted non-populist policies, it was because the crisis in these countries was so deep that even the short-term costs of sticking to populist policies became higher than the costs of adjustment' (1993: 57).

Secondly, institutional investors, while believing authoritarian regimes are more likely to choose their version of economic reform, demonstrate a clear preference for formulaic neo-liberal economic reforms prescribed by the IMF stabilization programs or the 'Washington consensus' (Williamson, 1990). In other words, the belief is that if countries fail to achieve desired economic results it is because they have not had the wherewithal to implement the reforms, and not that the particular brand of reform was flawed. As Bresser Pereira points out, 'Political scientists, when analyzing constraints on economic policies, usually accept as a given that economists (or the World Bank or the IMF) *know* which policies are to be adopted' (1993: 57). The evidence shows that this is true of institutional investors as they most often take for granted the nature of the reform to be implemented, and focus their analysis on the ability of the government to implement the prescribed reform. However, history has provided examples of the failure of many of these 'preferred' strategies. Remmer's study of IMF standby programs showed 'only a moderate correlation between the implementation of IMF prescriptions and the achievement of desired economic results' (1986). Bresser Pereira cites Brazil's Collor's Plan I as an example of a policy that failed because of its poor design rather than its lack of implementation (1993: 58). However, perhaps the most stunning examples have been in the series of crises that have rocked the emerging markets in the late 1990s. Mexico, the Asian NICs, Russia, and Brazil had all conformed to the prescriptions set out by investors and the IMF, often in the face of significant popular opposition. Moreover, even if IMF reforms *were* necessary but not sufficient for stabilization, these prescriptions appear to have failed to anticipate adequately and prepare enough for the probability of a balance of payments crisis in each country case. In fact, in some instances, IMF reforms may have inadvertently helped precipitate the investor selling frenzy. The inability of these reforms to prevent these economic and political catastrophes is a dilemma for the international financial community. Furthermore, although to date it is still relatively early to tell, it appears that countries with more established democratic institutions, such as Hong Kong, South Korea, Mexico, and Brazil, have better implemented reforms following their respective fiscal crises than more authoritarian regimes such as Malaysia and Indonesia.

If regime type does not matter, and democracies may even be better equipped to deal with after-crises reforms, what could perpetuate institutional investor preferences for authoritarian regimes and the implementation of one brand of neo-liberal reforms? Three reasons seem plausible. First, institutional investors and their analysts limit their macroeconomic analyses to aggregate annual, monthly, and weekly measures of economic statistics and corporate reports and, as a result, are not likely to incorporate evidence from the comparative political economy camp. The second related reason that large investors may discount this evidence is that their time horizons are so short. Although most emerging market funds managers warn those investing with them of the long-time horizons needed when investing in developing countries, they themselves are judged at least every quarter on their returns. The average annual turnover rate for emerging market funds listed by Reuters Money Network in June 1996, for instance, was 82 per cent. Of these 34 funds, only four had a turnover rate of less than 20 per cent. Some turnover rates were as high as 259 per cent.[11] As Matthew Merritt, director of emerging-markets strategy at ING Barings, puts it 'At best we have two to three years to show results...And mostly, it's quarter to quarter' (Mellow, 1998). Brady bond traders and currency speculators compound the problem of short-term time horizons as they pull money daily out of countries in the blink of an eye. As Barton Biggs of Morgan Stanley describes emerging market portfolio flows 'This money has all the conviction of a herd of wildebeest' (Makin, 1992: 184). Another large investor uses what he terms the 'cockroach theory' of investing:

> If a company holds up under his microscope, Webb [the fund manager] buys and holds until the criteria that sparked his faith is no longer applicable. Then he applies the cockroach theory: 'Where you find one, you'll find more' One bad indicator – a negative view from an analyst, for example – may mean a positive trend is about to reverse. 'We see a cockroach, we get out,' says Webb. That doesn't lead to long-term investing – Webb estimates that the fund's turnover rate is perhaps 200% (*Dow Jones News*, 16 October 1996: 2).

The evidence does not strongly support the belief that authoritarian regimes can offer better economic performance over the long term. However, the same economic performance over the long term means little to an investor who is reading economic indicators on a daily basis. In addition, portfolio investment grows not when economies are actually doing better over the longer term, but when other investors believe that *other* investors will believe these countries will show better numbers in the shorter term. More than a year is often an eternity in the life of fund or bond holding.

The implications of this short-term approach have already manifested themselves in the crises faced by Asia and parts of Latin America. Working within the confines of their profit-seeking modes, investors were unwilling to suffer through the showing of poor quarters and returns in order to ease, and perhaps alleviate, the currency crises which devastated many emerging markets in 1997 and 1998. In many ways, their dilemmas can be seen as the same as the problems faced in fostering international cooperation. For instance, if all investors agreed to extend their commitment to developing countries and maintain their investments through a possible crisis, this cooperation could alleviate the overselling that takes place due to early defection.

In addition, the preferences of institutional investors for stability over democracy appear to be supported by US foreign policy and many of the multilateral institutions. By the term 'democracy' here, I am referring to the institutional investors' perception of the term, which tends not to be very complicated. When a country has elections that appear to be relatively fair and free, civil liberties are not severely restricted, and political rights appear to mirror Western standards, investors are likely to perceive a country as democratic. What has been termed the 'Washington consensus' around economic reform, extends into the realm of political development. The argument that economic liberalization will usher in democratization has a strong backing in US foreign policy. The choice to ignore or downplay human rights issues in countries like China with great market potential is defended consistently by the argument that freer markets will eventually lead to democratization. This argument is also often buttressed by the corollary that political liberalization before economic liberalization can lead to disasters such as Russia. Some historical evidence supports this contention when one looks at the democratization in South Korea and Chile that followed the economic successes experienced under authoritarian regimes. So toleration of repressive regimes is often looked upon as a benevolent and wise rather than morally reprehensible and unwise.

Conclusions

This collection of preferences from the finance community leads to several conclusions. First, as any good financial analyst will point out, financial markets do not like uncertainty. Minimizing risk is paramount to an institutional investor and is one of the primary reasons they ventured into emerging markets in the first place. Studies have shown the low correlation between US markets and emerging markets, thus offering investors a venue for offsetting US investment risk. Although democracy, once solidly in place for long periods of time may offer less uncertainty, most emerging markets are still either in transitional stages of democracy or are still under authoritarian rule.

The shorter-term interest of portfolio capital investors and traders compounds the difficulties faced by emerging market countries to liberalize politically if most large investors will not tolerate the uncertainty of political transitions. In those political transitions, whether elections or whole regime changes, they inevitably signal uncertainty and are not likely to bode well with fund managers wanting to show the best numbers for each quarter. And, even though evidence suggests that democracy may indeed help stabilize politics and economics in the long run, it is unlikely that the inherent short-sighted bias of most bond and equity market investors would be willing to wait it out.

However, in some cases this preference for stability need not always favor increased authoritarianism, as Elizondo argues (1999). He suggests that in the case of Mexico in the 1990s, investors believed that political stability would be best preserved through fairer elections and a loosening of Partido Revolucionario Institucional (PRI) power. He notes the financial market's positive reaction to the election of Partido Revolucionario Democratico (PRD) candidate, Cuauhtemoc Cardenas, as Mexico's city's first non-PRD mayor since 1929 (Elizondo, 145). However, it could be argued, investors were perhaps more aware of Mexico's political problems than other developing countries because of its proximity to the US border and the widely publicized Chiapas uprisings and political assassinations.

In addition, the positive reaction of the financial markets to the election of a PRD candidate to a mayoral office is arguably different than the election of a PRD candidate to the presidency. If the PRD, of the moderate left, were in charge of national economic policy, for instance, the reaction of the markets could be quite different.

Nonetheless, this event does provide some evidence that political liberalization may appear the more stabilizing path to investors if potential threats to the status quo power are publicized enough, perceived as credible, and threaten to destabilize more if unattended. However, as this chapter demonstrates, a good number of institutional investment professionals perceive transition to democracy as a risky proposition.

4
Expression of Preferences: Systems of Investor Knowledge

Chapter 3 discussed institutional investor preferences for stability and the possibility of the consequent devaluing of democracy. This chapter and Chapter 5 will look at the systems by which this preference for stability becomes homogenized and expressed to the governments of developing countries in search of capital. Focusing on two phenomena, investor organization (Chapter 4) and investor activism (Chapter 5), the argument will be made that investors have become better organized, more skilled, and bolder in communicating their expectations to developing markets. Moreover, as the amount of capital going into the hands of institutional investors increases, leverage over their prospective and current holdings increases. The systemic factors shaping emerging financial markets are understood through an examination of different levels of collaboration taking place within the international financial community. First, the shared belief in complying with neo-liberal tenets leads to the uniformity of doctrine adhered to by institutional investors. Secondly, goals particular to large investors impose another systemic constraint in which the profit-motive reigns supreme and is an important departure from the systemic constraints set by official development assistance. Thirdly, the specific forms of information and communication pertaining to emerging financial markets have profound effects on the way prospective investors and developing country governments perceive economic and political success. Fourthly, the particular characteristics of financial markets are important in understanding how global emerging market funds are distributed. Fifthly, organizations, both governmental and non-governmental, provide an important tool for institutional investors to communicate with emerging market countries through a third party. Industry trade associations as well as institutions like the IMF and World Bank are critical spaces in which investors collaborate to achieve their objectives. These five systemic determinants of investor and emerging market behavior do not necessarily entail a direct expression of preference by individual institutional investors, but are vital in exercising power nonetheless. Chapter 5 will address the more intentional forms of collaboration by discussing more overt coordination and investor activism, or the effort of investors to shape directly the political and economic events in emerging market countries.

Institutional investors and the structuring of capitalism for developing countries

Perhaps one of the most vital aspects of a free market is the degree to which it operates fairly, not subjected to any one individual or group of individuals. As Chapter 2 suggested, the inefficiencies of the international financial markets in which emerging stock markets participate support a system of capital allocation in which institutional investors possess potential political power in developing countries. How this power is organized and ultimately exercised is examined through the following five types of collaboration: (i) ideological (neoliberal consensus); (ii) intra-firm (firm-level systemic): (iii) inter-firm (information gathering, organization, and exchange); (iv) market-level (market phenomenon); and (v) institutional (institutions).

Neo-liberal consensus

In the fairest of securities markets, macroeconomic and political risk analyses are derived from a shared economic doctrine and its valuation of certain political systems. Thus, even at the most general and random level, it can be argued that a natural conformity emanates from international institutional investors' shared neoliberal conditioning. While this is something different than a concerted effort to collaborate, it nonetheless begins to demarcate the boundaries of the finance industry's system of knowledge. The pervasiveness of this shared ideology makes it difficult to argue against the neoclassical economic tenet that it is the capital market that decides who gets what, rather than the owners of capital. The increase in private capital flows versus non-private does not drastically alter politics at this level of collaboration since neoliberal economics and politics permeate most of the policies of the declining multilateral and bilateral official capital contributors. However, several factors have contributed to the strengthening of the neoliberal doctrines.

The strengthening of the belief that free market ideology is best has happened in the last decade of the twentieth century as the political and economic debates about development changed dramatically. The success of the East Asian economic miracles beginning in the mid-1980s and the failure of communism in the Soviet Union eliminated many of the arguments against liberal market reform. Or, as one economist put it, 'The emerging market countries watched the great ideological contest of the Cold War for decades. ... Now they know which system is best' (Marotta, 1996: 1). The larger debate over the relationship between economic growth and democracy incorporated the impact of these two enormous political events. The question of *whether* countries should adopt economic liberalization shifted to *how* countries should implement liberalization.

The shift in finance sourcing for developing countries is part of this change, as well as resulting from the debt crisis, the advent of fiscal conservatism, explosion of pension funds, and the vast technological changes in the finance industry. However, the change in finance sourcing from governments and multilateral institutions to private investors has also constituted and intensified the shift in thinking, from *whether* to *how* market reforms. In addition to this narrowing of choice of economic systems, the shift from government to private financing has also reduced the question of *how* to a relatively homogenized process.

One element contributing to this homogenization is the small world in which international finance operates. One frequently heard comment by emerging markets analysts and traders has been how small the world is in which they operate. A senior economist and emerging markets analyst at one of the leading US banks commented that 'all traders know each other anyway'.[1] This was the second part of a response to a question about verifying advanced information of a Moody's upgrade. The first part indicated that another trader would first telephone his contact at Moody's, and then some traders at other firms to confirm this potentially money making inside information. Another source from a German bank commented on the same phenomenon by stating 'all these guys know each other anyway'.[2] These anecdotes are even more convincing when one looks at the institutions of higher learning from which they acquired the bulk of their learning about theories and neoliberal doctrines.

The private sector side of international finance and the public sector domain of national economic policies are often intricately linked. For instance, many of the most powerful economic policymakers in emerging market countries received their training from one of the few top-notch business training grounds for executives in the US. For instance, Guillermo Ortiz, Mexico's renowned finance minister and later governor of the central bank, did his graduate work at Stanford's Business School. He also served as executive director of the IMF from 1984 to 1988. Chile's finance minister, Eduardo Aninat, was educated at Harvard as was Domingo Cavallo, Argentina's finance minister renowned for implementing sweeping free-market reforms. Chile's President Ricardo Lagos received a PhD in economics from Duke University. El Salvador's finance minister, Manual Hinds, received his degree in economics from Northwestern University. He then served as a private consultant for the World Bank before returning to El Salvador. Hafeez Pasha, Deputy Chairman of Government of Pakistan's Planning Commisssion and previously Federal Minister of Commerce, received an MA from Cambridge and a PhD in economics from Stanford. Thailand's Minister of Finance, Tarrin Nimmanahaeminda, received his BA from Harvard and obtained an MBA in finance at Stanford as well. His Deputy Minister of Finance, Dr. Pisit Leeahtam, was an economist and assistant to the Executive Director at the IMF before his tenure at the ministry. Suharto, in the midst of trying to salvage Indonesia's economy and his political tenure following the Asian Crisis of 1997, fired his central bank governor and replaced him with the US-educated Sjahiril Sabirin. Arminio Fraga, Brazil's latest central bank head, was trained at Princeton.

This phenomenon of similar educational backgrounds also happens at the level of the multilateral development agencies like the IMF and World Bank. For instance, at the 1998 World Bank/IMF Annual Meeting, the seminar on 'Building Better Banking: Banking System Fragility' consisted of nine experts, eight of whom received their doctorates from a prominent US business or economics school. Four of the nine members of this committee trained or taught at

Stanford University. One scholar attributed developing countries' shift to market-oriented policies to the US training of government leaders, stating: 'Frequently, the impetus for change has come from local economists who were trained at the U.S. universities: former President Carlos Salinas in Mexico, [and] the 'Chicago Boys' in Chile' (Marotta, 1996: 1–2). In addition to these educational similarities, many government economists and institutional investors share similar career experiences.[3] Following the devaluation and subsequent slide of the real in 1999, Brazil's President Cardoso appointed Armino Fraga, manager of the Soros Fund, as central bank president. Nicholas Brady, former US treasury secretary, runs Darby Overseas Investments, a private emerging markets investment firm in Washington DC. One of Brady's managing partners, Richard Frank, was a former managing director at the World Bank. Robert Rubin, former US Secretary of the Treasury, instrumental in mapping the future international architecture and directing IMF policy, works at Citigroup.

The pre-eminence of Western business schools like Stanford in the backgrounds of emerging market finance ministers suggests a shared conformity to the classic neoliberal leanings of business school academia. Furthermore, the world of international finance is compressed further by the practice of governments, financial firms, and multilateral lending agencies of drawing their experts from a small number of prominent schools. This practice presumably also feeds off itself as new graduates are often hired by alumni, thus perpetuating the consensus around a particular vision of international markets.

Firm-level systemic: profit-motives replace aid politics

The next possible level of coordination is also at a systemic level but at that of the firm, or in the case of governmental entities, the bureaucracy. The systemic differences are best characterized by the differing goals between private capital and multilateral lending. Although coinciding at times, the goals of private capital investments are usually quite different than multilateral bank lending or official development assistance. For instance, the purpose of multilateral bank lending and foreign aid was not or at least not until recently, explicitly for the rate of return.[4] The criteria for choosing appropriate candidates and the methods of disciplining capital recipients are changing as countries are judged more like commodities or public corporations than vehicles for development, resource distribution, or geo-strategic positioning. Choosing a country according to private incentives is different in that private capital gives most to those with the highest expected return rather than the highest need. Moreover, in spite of all the criticism of the multilateral lending institutions and their linkages with private capital interests, their mission, at least professed is, to have humanitarian and democratic goals as well.

However, it is important to acknowledge the well-documented flaws of foreign development assistance. Foreign aid donors have been criticized for decades and many of these criticisms have come in the form of comparisons between donor policies and politics. Many of these critical comparisons can be found in the works of Browne, 1990; Feinberg and Raqtchik, 1991 and Griffith, 1991. Throughout these works aid donors are judged by many criteria but all share one main point of comparison; the degree to which foreign aid is motivated by donor self-interest. One of the most consistent critics of foreign multilateral assistance, Cheryl Payer, suggests that there is little difference between private direct investment and official foreign loans and grants when it comes to evaluating the detrimental effects of foreign capital. According to Payer, both types of capital share the 'objective of taking out of a country more than is brought in' (Payer, 1991: xi). With this criticism in mind, it is worth looking at some of the similarities between foreign aid and institutional investments.

The allocative structures for foreign aid and private investment have both similarities and differences. If we take foreign aid at its worst, it is motivated primarily by self-interest on the part of the donor and tends to flow to those areas that will benefit the donor country economically, strategically and/or politically. In particular, the practice of tying aid to the recipient's purchase of products and services from the donor country parallels the return on investment that private investment seeks. Another similarity is the tendency to direct capital to areas that are donor-friendly and provide, or indicate future provision of, some political or strategic benefit to the donor. In the case of foreign aid, this may come in the form of an alliance or land for an army base. Private investors may be promised proprietary rights to sell a government bond overseas or an easing of financial restrictions.

Other more obvious similarities between foreign aid and private investment include the direction of flows from developed to developing countries, the concentration of flows to medium-level developing countries rather than lower-level developing countries, and the underlying valuation of neoliberal market reform and structures. However, whatever the drawbacks of bilateral and multilateral aid, there are some important distinctions between aid agencies and institutional investment firms that suggest that aid may have more likely led to fostering human rights and democracy than private capital.

Although foreign aid and private institutional investment may share the motivation of self-interest and tendencies described above; foreign aid may have been a better catalyst for democracy than private institutional investment. First, foreign aid, although perhaps motivated by strategic and economic self-interest, has at least often been accompanied by the normative goal of assisting developing countries overcome poverty and underdevelopment. Whether real or a pretense, the goal of helping developing countries achieve political and economic development, coexisted with the goals of donor self-interest. This union, at the very least, did allow for the barrage of criticism against foreign aid donors. These criticisms often led them to come to terms with policies that allocated, for instance, to dictators, human rights violators, and polluters.

Another important difference is between the organizational features of the foreign aid bureaucracy and the regime of institutional investors. Although this chapter has focused on the coherency and coordination of institutional investors, crucial differences between the two systems make the organization of foreign aid allocation more conducive to global accountability and scrutiny. Foreign aid has the organizational structures of the multilateral and bilateral aid bureaucracies. Within these structures exist well-established systems of tracking foreign aid expenditures, development projects, and breakdowns of sector spending. In other words, it was, and is, relatively simple to know how much the US, or any other country is giving and loaning to developing countries, which projects aid has been supporting, and to which sectors the aid is flowing. In contrast, no formal institution exists through which portfolio flows are organized. It is very difficult to track the daily trading of international institutional investors within EMCs. Daily records from emerging market stock exchanges and the daily prices of individual stocks within these exchanges are obtainable, but it is extremely difficult to separate domestic investors from foreign. This makes it nearly impossible to determine who is investing where on a daily basis. This lack of data on the flow of private capital into EMCs makes it more difficult to hold investors accountable.

Foreign aid has institutional systems of accountability, with varying degrees of effectiveness, which monitor foreign aid expenditures. National accounting systems, the Organization of Economic Cooperation and Development (OECD), and the World Bank are some of the more prominent institutions, which gather and disseminate information, formulate reports for public consumption, and make comparisons between foreign aid donors. In the world of global finance, no international entity or nation-state can be held accountable for the actions of institutional investors. Furthermore, no organization can adequately oversee the increasingly rapid and vast amount of capital that flows throughout the electronic networks of today.

However, even if such a formal accounting system were to exist for international investments, it is unrealistic to believe that the type of scrutiny would be similar. Differing expectations for foreign aid and institutional investment would prevent the usage of similar principles by which to judge capital flows to developing countries. Although foreign aid donors have probably had an implicit expectation that official development assistance in someway benefit the donor's domestic status, it is not grounded in an explicit primary objective for rate of return on grants or loans. In order to survive, private investors in the emerging markets must maintain the primary objective of making money. Foreign aid, while perhaps imbued with donor self-interest, also often contains a primary motivation to assist developing countries. Germany, Sweden and the Netherlands have established aid conditionality on the observance of human rights and others have expressed 'concern for democratic pluralism and rule of law'.[5] Other donors, such as the United States in the 1980s, show a '[perverse] relationship between aid and human rights violations' (UN, 1994: 76). Multilateral lenders in general also do not carry a good record for supporting countries that have more democratic institutions in place (UN, 1994: 76). However, even in the face of a poor record for supporting democratic institutions and human rights, foreign aid has been at least subjected to this criticism. Not surprisingly, the expectation exists that foreign aid will help rather than hinder political democracy. The United Nations, the OECD, and the World Bank collect data to track donors' records in this regard. Emerging market investors are subject to a different and more singular scrutiny; the rate of return.

These investors, explicitly seeking rate of return and risk minimization, will value most a country's ability to implement and maintain neoliberal economic reforms, even in the face of significant popular opposition. Private investors, as we saw in Chapter 3, do not often demonstrate a preference for political democracy but rather for political stability. With these points in mind, is it possible that the past supremacy of foreign aid organizations may have been better for political democracy than the present dominance of the institutional investor system of preferences?

Information gathering, organization, and exchange

The manner in which knowledge about the emerging markets is gathered, organized, and disseminated throughout the financial industry, represents one aspect of how the neoliberal norm is proliferated and strengthened by those most privileged by it, the institutional investors. In addition, because of increases in communications technology, the increasing amounts of information available about the financial markets is often used as evidence that financial markets are efficient (see Chapter 2), and investors are equal in their access to information. One way for setting up a framework for understanding how international capital distribution is systemically coordinated by the norms of institutional investors, is to sort out what informational signals influence investors and how these signals are gathered, organized, and transmitted. For instance, it is important to determine if cues to institutional investors are signals derived from independent analysis of macroeconomic statistics and risk, or if investors take cues from common sources and/or from each other. Chapter 2 demonstrated the existence of a departure from market efficiency in emerging markets and, implies that, given the differences in trading between the New York and London exchanges, institutional investors do have information systems that influence their investment choices. In a securities market, the more investors and diversity of risk preferences that are added to the market, the more stable the market will become. This commonly accepted view, that the emerging stock markets volatility will decrease as more investors are added to the pool, is based on the assumption that these new investors will have access to independent information and that they will make their judgments independently of one another. In other words, '... that differences in expectations, risk preferences, and liquidity needs among investors are purely random' (IMF, 1995: 29). As one approaches perfect market competition, one also assumes that no single investor will be able to influence the market in its favor or that no group will be able to collaborate to accomplish this. Research indicates that in a market where there is a low number of investors and a few large investors with inside information, the market will be subject to greater fluctuations in price as a result of the ability of the large investors to manipulate the market (IMF, 1995: 29). The phrase, 'greater fluctuations in price,' while sounding fairly benign in this context, can mean the crashing of a currency or stock market in a day as several emerging markets experienced in Asia in 1997, Russia in 1997, and Mexico in 1994. As we have seen, these 'price fluctuations' have profound political implications as well.

The idea that institutional investors derive their information from common sources indicates a level of coordination on their part, albeit not necessarily intentional. Informational coordination takes place on three levels. First, the gathering of primary information is performed by a limited number of entities and is often subjective, given the relative dearth of official financial information available on developing markets. Secondly, organizing information on the emerging markets occurs through processes of standardization, categorization, and systemization. Certain countries make it into the charmed circle of emerging markets, others don't. Thirdly, the informal and formal networks of communication within the finance industry shrink and homogenize information putting even more power in the hands of the experts.

Gathering information

Very few corporations or organizations have representatives domiciled in developing countries for the purposes of collecting information relevant to investors. As discussed in Chapter 2, even large investors rely on the relatively few experts in the emerging markets.

Information gathering on corporations, political climate, and investment regulations, whether done by foreign analysts domiciled in EMCs or managers traveling there, can be expensive so utilizing the information and expertise acquired by others is commonplace. In addition, most investors use government published numbers on macroeconomic statistics although these have been frequently criticized for their inaccuracy, particularly in the areas of real inflation rates. The Internet has begun to provide more information to investors but is still limited in its capacity to collect viable statistics and often uses the numbers configured by the government or one of the few large institutions collecting pertinent data.

One good example of the limited utilization of information sources on EMCs is the power credit agencies wield over the developing world. Bond investors and foreign direct investors, for instance, have always relied heavily on two credit agencies, Moody's and Standard and Poor's, for their assessments of investability. However, the initiation of pension funds and mutual fund capital into emerging markets has magnified the power of Moody's and Standard and Poor's. Called the 'bloodhounds' for investors, these agencies led the way for many mutual funds and pension funds to invest in the emerging markets as they upgraded their credit ratings for many of these countries in the mid-1990s (Friedman, 1999: 91). Many mutual funds and pension funds have mandates or policies that prohibit investments in vehicles with below investment grade ratings. US pension funds, for instance, by law are required to invest only in investment grade securities. As the status of many emerging markets changed to investment grade in the mid-1990s, funds began pouring into these countries (IMF, 1998: 23). However, 'as the credit ratings of a number of emerging markets declined below investment grade from July 1997, these new institutional investors either sharply reduced their purchases of emerging market securities or eliminated their holdings' (IMF, 1998: 23). The centralization of credit information within these two agencies shrinks the pool of information used by institutional investors.

This reliance on these two agencies also can have far-reaching effects on the countries rated. In early September 1998, Moody's downgraded Brazil and Venezuela and precipitated a financial collapse in their markets. Moody's lowered their creditworthiness not because their fundamental domestic economy had changed, but because the Asian Crisis had adversely affected their international financial positions. Ernesto Martinez-Alas, a senior analyst at Moody's, confirms this as he states after the downgrade, 'We're indicating the conditions that affect the countries have dramatically changed for the worse and that is reflected in the lower ratings' (Bussey, 1998: 2). This tendency to downgrade because of reliance on international funds and other factors exogenous to a country's economic fundamentals can be common. Michel Camdessus, then managing director for the IMF, commented on the Brazilian and Venezuelan cases:

> This is not the first occasion where actions by a rating agency do not reflect a change in the medium- and long-term prospects of a country but rather recognition, after the fact, that the country, or the countries, are currently suffering deterioration of their external environment (Bussey, 1998: 4).

The decision to lower ratings is normally made by a committee at the individual rating agencies. These committees typically base their decisions on a report compiled by one in-office person and one field person (Bussey, 1998: 2). Given the already heavy reliance on the two largest, Moody's and Standard and Poor's, the two-person report narrows even further the information transmitted to large investors.

Unsurprisingly, these credit agencies have been criticized for their short-sighted, biased, and self-serving reports. Teodoro Petkoff, Venezuelan Planning Minister, asked Latin American countries to denounce these agencies so that investors would no longer use 'the biased reports of agencies like Moody's and Standard and Poor's' (Bussey, 1998: 1). The finance ministers of Mexico and Brazil, Jose Angel Gurria and Pedro Malan respectively, suggested that Latin America 'was paying the price for the failure by the rating agencies to foresee the Asian crisis' (Bussey, 1998: 2). Although the IMF and World Bank have addressed the issue of credit agency power, these two rating agencies and their report processes still determine the international perception of country creditworthiness.

*Standardization and categorization: the emerging markets
investment category*

The manner in which investors have created a hierarchical system of arranging the profit potential for developing countries can be observed through an examination of the emerging-markets investment category and its effects on the developing countries. The term 'emerging market' originated in 1986 when the World Bank's International Finance Corporation (IFC) was given the task of creating a fund for capital market development for developing countries. One of their duties was to define what constituted an emerging market. Officially, countries are categorized as 'emerging' if they fall into the low- or middle-income World Bank classifications, those countries that have per capita average annual incomes of less than a specified amount, usually somewhere around US$10,000.[6] However, the definition of an emerging market most often refers to those countries that have been chosen by the financial community as worthy investment options. The absence of a suitable financial infrastructure or the presence of unacceptable economic indicators often prohibits the entrance of countries into the world of portfolio investments. In addition, the geographic position of a country can keep them classified as an emerging market despite their average per capita incomes surpassing the World Bank-specified ceiling.[7] This phenomenon has the added impact of potentially inhibiting the entrance of other poorer countries from making it to this 'privileged status'. Here it should be noted that, although this book questions the increased reliance on private portfolio flows to developing countries, this does not imply that *not* receiving these flows is necessarily a good thing. For instance, in the case of this categorization, if all developing countries were given equal visibility for investment opportunities, this would tend to improve the efficiency and fairness of capital distribution. It may also have the added benefit of inhibiting the speculative bubbles formed by asset concentration within a few markets.

The practice of choosing some countries for emerging market status has some of its origins in the International Finance Corporation. According to the IFC, emerging markets officially includes all countries in Latin America; Africa; Asia, with the exception of New Zealand, Australia and Japan; some in Southern Europe, specifically Greece, Turkey, and Portugal; all countries in Eastern Europe including Russia, the Ukraine and other parts of the former Soviet empire. However, at the beginning of 1992 the IFC began to publish a list of countries that were considered 'investable,' practically decreasing the number of emerging markets. An IFC index of emerging markets also now exists for which countries must qualify. Table 4.1 shows a

Table 4.1   Market capitalization of emerging stock markets, 1985–1997

Country	Market capitalization		% change
	1985	1997	
Argentina	1,301.3	35,141.84	2,601
Brazil	11,730.47	102,964.53	778
Chile	931.56	44,497.78	4,677
Colombia	300.67	11,451.92	3,709
Greece	276.15	16,255.06	5,786
India	3,965.44	50,856.13	1,182
Indonesia	1	13,553.49	1,355,249
Jordan	1,322.92	3,261.18	147
Korea	2,400.59	25,157.21	948
Malaysia	8,854.92	45,910.56	418
Mexico	1,395.33	108,940.67	7,708
Nigeria	1,499.07	2,553.79	70
Pakistan	584.08	5,978.88	924
Philippines	265.64	18,650.24	6,921
Portugal	1	24,745.01	2,474,401
Taiwan, China	3,818.99	153,175.76	3,911
Thailand	1,097.32	10,921.17	895
Turkey	1	33,732.35	3,373,135
Venezuela	598.26	9,138.38	1,427
Zimbabwe	169.5	1,123.01	563

Source: IFC Emerging Markets Database, 1999

listing of the core countries that the IFC consistently reported statistics for since 1985, and their increases in market capitalization between 1985 and 1997.

The IFC list of 'eligible' countries represents a very basic level by which capital distribution is organized in categories. This process of binary categorization – investable and non-investable – is unlike sovereign lending because the ranking of countries takes place exclusively according to economic risk. Countries are divided into acceptable and unacceptable risk categories based on investment grade rankings. Countries without the capacity to realize rates of production and consumption higher than other countries can be deprived of needed capital. The terms are also defined according to investors in this new ranking system. Political risk refers mostly to the chances a government will nationalize, change tax incentives, or give concessions to labor unions. Civil unrest becomes important only if it holds the threat of disrupting these investment safeguards. Capital invested in emerging countries is no longer attached to political or strategic goals as often accompanied the lending or foreign aid from sovereign nations. Instead, institutional investors operate with the expectations of not only growth within a country, but more growth than other countries can deliver. This has created a competitive atmosphere among developing countries as they scramble to get a portion of the US$1 trillion traded daily on the foreign exchange market (Smith, 1995: 44).

This process extends beyond the IFC. Publications read by the finance community, such as *The Economist*, the *Financial Times*, and the *Wall Street Journal* have sections reporting on what they consider emerging markets. *The Economist* lists only 25 countries on the last page section entitled 'Emerging-Market Indicators'. The *Financial Times* carries 33 countries (all those listed in *The Economist*, plus Morocco, Nigeria, Jordan, Pakistan, Sri Lanka, Slovakia, and Zimbabwe) in its section 'World Markets at a Glance'. The *Wall Street Journal* runs a section entitled the 'Dow Jones Global Indexes' in which statistics from exchanges in only 14 developing countries are reported. In 1997 the *Wall Street Journal* featured a special section on world business called 'Money Hungry' in which they noted the existence of what they termed 'the billionaire's club' of developing countries (Lehner, 1997: R1). In 1996, only 25 out of 150 developing countries qualified for membership because of their ability to attract over US$1 billion in foreign capital. Twelve of these recipients received 73 per cent of private capital flows in 1996 (Lehner, 1997: R4). The inclination of the business press to include only the biggest recipients of private capital flows reinforces their success at the potential detriment of other countries competing for these funds. By strengthening name recognition on a daily, weekly, and monthly basis, the business press helps buttress one of the principle elements of investor confidence, familiarity. In addition, the emphasis on categorization based on the ability to attract foreign investors diminishes the relative merit of what individual countries are doing with their economic policies. Countries like Bangladesh that have followed the economic reform formulas set up by the investment community can still experience legitimacy problems because of public image.[8] The emphasis on larger emerging markets also implies that smaller markets will suffer from lack of inclusion in these indices, as well as insufficient media coverage of their economic progress. Excluding the majority of the developing countries from these indices also may impact an excluded country's impetus to collect and disseminate accurate macroeconomic statistics. The effects wrought by the processes of inclusion and exclusion are also intensified by the growing use of index funds for emerging markets. Indexing, or the passive management of securities, is investing in the securities that are represented in various proportions within a particular index. Investors do not actively trade stocks and often premise their choice of this strategy on the assumption that an index of emerging market stocks will do as well as an active manager. In addition, index funds cost the investor far less because of manager fee and transaction cost reductions. The costs of active management, discussed in Chapter 2, can be very high because of the high costs of travel, research, and trading in an emerging market. Thus, index funds have become increasingly attractive options for some investors. Jeff Davis, vice president of global structured products at State Street Global Advisors in Boston commented 'We had to beg, borrow, and steal just to get our first US$30 million for our original IFC [index] fund' (Rademan, 1996: 83). Within three years, the fund had over US$5 billion in passive emerging market funds (Rademan, 1996: 84).

At first glance, it appears as if these funds offer a rather objective way to invest in emerging markets. Utilizing an index compiled according to country, industry, and corporate weightings appears relatively apolitical as the inclusion and level of investments depends upon their relative weight within the index, rather than the more subjective assessment of individual managers. However, upon scrutiny, the construction process of the three major indexes reveals the inherent biases of the process and the reinforcement of existing institutional norms and preferences. The IFC, Morgan Stanley Capital International (MSCI-EMF) and ING Barings Emerging Markets Index (BEMI) construct the three most utilized indexes. Each of these indexes employs a different methodology to choose which countries will be selected, which securities to include, how to weight industries and countries within the index, and how to account for such things as investability constraints and cross-shareholdings. However, each index ends up with a very similar list of countries. 'The three providers use different criteria to define which markets are 'emerging' but nonetheless end up with quite similar lists' (Rademan, 1996: 84). For instance, country selection, although implying the inclusion of the 'emerging markets,' actually defines emerging markets in a more limited way than the World Bank. As previously mentioned, according to the World Bank the official criteria for a market to be emerging is that they have an per capita annual income of less than US$10,000. Thus, theoretically, all developing countries should be included in this category – but all the indexes eliminate those countries with poor investment potential. The Barings and Morgan Stanley indexes further limit country selection only to those countries with certain levels of economic growth and financial market liquidity. This fact again leaves the list of emerging markets ranging from approximately 27 to 19 countries (Rademan, 1996: 84).[9] In addition to the limited number of countries permitted in these indexes, the indexes also exclude certain securities. The ING Barings index, for instance, includes only the most liquid, blue-chip stocks and these must be covered by their own analysts. The IFC and MSCI also evaluate securities based on the tradeability of a stock basing their choices on liquidity and the amount of shares outstanding, or float. ING Barings further weights its choices for the index by limiting the evaluation of float only to the number of shares that are available to foreigners. The other indexes might also eliminate companies that have large market capitalization but limited stock available to foreigners because of government or corporate restrictions.

All of these restrictions; based on factors like a country's stock market maturity and breadth, a company's number of outstanding shares, and government regulation on foreign stock ownership; have whittled down these indexes to a relatively small number of companies. The ING Barings index for example, contained only 417 securities worldwide. The IFC and MSCI, with freer criteria than ING Barings, still only included 1,116 and 868 respectively.[10]

However, even though these indexes represent only a very small portion of the available investment opportunities in developing countries, the index makers can wield a great deal of power. The *Institutional Investor* reports: 'As international money managers' interest in passive, or indexed, equity investing in these markets has grown in the past couple of years, so too has the power of the index makers' (Rademan, 1996: 82).

This means that these index makers can move markets. For instance, one day in 1996 the IFC caused a 5 per cent increase in the Chilean stock market by giving the country a heavier weighting in its index (Rademan, 1996: 82). In addition, the 'MSCI contributed to a 15 percent spike on the Taipei Stock Exchange after it announced that Taiwan was to be included in its prime index' (Rademan, 1996: 82–3). One of the reasons indexes possess this ability to move markets is their influence over active managers. Like most money managers, emerging market fund analysts compete with the major benchmarks in their field. In the US, beating the Standard and Poor (S&P) index is an often-heard goal among domestic investors. Similarly, the emerging market managers strive to outperform these major indexes. The use of these indexes as a yardstick, however, reinforces the status quo patterns of country and stock selections used by the index. For instance, if suddenly the indexes added a 15 per cent weighting for India, active fund managers would be pressured to up their own weightings in India. One manager claims 'active managers call it [indexing] a ball and chain' because of the aversion these managers have of deviating too far off index selections and weightings for fear of under-performing it (Rademan, 1996: 6). Conversely, these managers, both active and passive, have influence over the index compilers, further reinforcing the status quo boundaries drawn by large investment firms. Index compilers, in constant contact with passive and active managers, seek advice on particular equities and various indexing dilemmas. Resolving indexing problems stemming from political occurrences like Hong Kong's return to China and Malaysia's order for companies to delist from Singapore's stock exchange are two examples in which index compilers have turned to managers for direction.[11] This intercommunication among index compilers and money managers helps further solidify the norms by which international finance operates. These norms are then buttressed by the ability of indexes to move the markets. Emerging market countries and corporations courting these index makers are understandably attentive to the preferences expressed by them. Chapter 6 addresses the degree of some of this attentiveness by looking at a couple of policy measures enacted by emerging markets in order to gain a place on the indexes.

Investors' use of country categorization by the IFC, business press, and/or indexes appears to intensify after periods of economic crisis in one or more of the established emerging market countries. Investment risk itself tends to spread more easily throughout emerging markets following a crisis because of the propensity for investors to lump developing countries into the same investment category. Phrases like the 'Asian contagion' and the 'domino effect' have been used to describe this tendency. As a single-country crisis exacerbates the perceived, and often self-fulfilling, investment risk in other markets, investors tend toward safer havens. As one annual report of an emerging market mutual fund reports:

> This developed market liquidity will have great difficulty finding its way back to the "vulnerable" emerging markets.... In short, the separation between the "haves" and "have-nots" witnessed in 1998 will persist, and perhaps even widen in 1999; this process in the emerging markets universe is not unlike what has taken place in th US stock market between the mega-cap nifty fifty stocks (the haves) and the small cap or industrial commodity stocks (the have nots) (Meyer and Skov, 1999).

As a result of the above assessment, this fund overweighted emerging markets like Greece, Israel, and parts of Eastern Europe while underweighting Latin America and South Africa. This fund's strategy after the Asian Crisis was to 'tilt our portfolio toward high quality markets and sectors with fundamental underpinnings' (Meyer and Skol, 1999). While perhaps rational on the part of the portfolio managers, this propensity to associate risk categorically according to region can also become a self-fulfilling prophecy as investors must move out of countries they think other investors will avoid.

Communication networks

The close ties between investors become even closer when one examines the communications networks that link investors with one another. It is safe to say that large investors are in almost constant contact with other large investors. Publications, conferences, computer networks, radio communication systems, and television channels provide a free flow of information among these investors and those interested in what they are doing.

Publications targeting the finance community often encourage copycat behavior and promote the interests of large investors. Every industry has its common sources of information and the finance industry is no exception. The plethora of surveys and publications serves as medium of intercommunication between investors. Some of the most visible are *Institutional Investor, Barron's, The Economist,* and the *Financial Times.* However, there are also more specialized publications which target pension managers, bankers, and endowment fund managers. One of the main functions of these publications is to report on the preferences of the leaders in the field.

An interesting means by which these publications encourage investors to follow others are the competitions in which a favorite analyst is ranked in a particular field. *Institutional Investor* is perhaps most well known for its annual announcements of the 'Best Latin American Fund Manager' or the 'Best Emerging Markets Analyst'. Noting the winners' accomplishments in terms of their overall annual returns, or the realization of some of their unique predictions, these competitions single out individuals for investors to follow. Even retail managers are typically aware of a top analyst's thoughts on particular industries or countries. In other words, it is a common occurrence to hear that 'so-and-so' is recommending 'such-and-such'.

In addition to the proliferation of expert opinions through select publications, many corporations hold conferences to share information and discuss investment strategies for the future. These conferences provide institutional managers and their followers a forum to discuss which countries hold the most promise for the coming year. Barron's Roundtable conference, Salomon Smith Barney's Annual Closed-End Country Funds conference, and Crédit Lyonnais' Asia Investors' Forum are examples of such conferences held for institutional investors. At Salomon Smith Barney's, for instance, the top institutional investors in emerging markets are invited to share with each other their opinions and information about emerging market investments. As stated in one invitation 'the conference should appeal to institutional investors, in particular pension funds, insurance companies, private banks, hedge funds, and private client managers' (Salomon Smith Barney's invitation to a conference held in 1998). Detailed reports of the conference are then made available to the public, thus extending the reach of these top managers' opinions. Crédit Lyonnais Securities Asia began to hold an annual conference on investing in Asia in 1994. The 'Asia Investor's Forum' was held in May of 1995 and demonstrated the clear impact of these conferences on emerging stock markets. After 400 fund managers responsible for over US$3 trillion attended the conference, Asian markets 'posted their biggest gains in more than a year' (Sender, 1995: 66).[12] The gains were remarkable:

Hong Kong led the pack with a 10.6% surge, Jakarta and Manila jumped more than 8% each, and Thailand rose 6%. Many of the Asian companies that gave presentations saw their share prices soar. After executives from Indonesia's Lippo Bank concluded their remarks, the bank's shares rose 27% (Sender, 1995: 67).

A gathering of such large investors can have profound effects on capital flowing into developing countries. In the above instance, the consensus helped inflows increase.[13] However, the sentiment can work against countries as well. For instance, at the conference, '... enthusiasm was not uniform. The taste for anything to do with China has soured' (Sender, 1995: 66). In addition to these efforts to exchange information in person, most institutional investors have highly developed technological information services for discovering on a minute-by-minute basis what other institutional investors are doing. These computer networks can be grouped into two categories, inter- and intra-firm. The computer networks that connect investors are elaborate and few in number. The three primary distributors of financial information to the larger brokerage firms are Reuters, Bloomberg, and Dow Jones Industrial News Service. These linkages provide retail and institutional brokers the same information on political and economic statistics, mutual fund holdings, and insider trading activity.

The intra-firm network firms typically relay information between analysts, traders, and brokers. A large investment firm, for instance, posts it's analysts' top picks according to industry, market capitalization, and/or country location. Thus, even if the firm is a retail firm with thousands of financial consultants around the country, it is likely that their investment choices will be heavily influenced by their firm's research recommendations. Furthermore, it is relatively easy and commonplace for large firms to list the ratings of stocks from other firm's analysts. In international equity investing, including the emerging markets, brokerage companies are aware of each other's international portfolio weightings. In addition, announcements of a large investor's re-grading of a country are prevalent.

Similar to the computer networks available to international investors, the opinions and preferences of the large institutional investors are disseminated through broadcast mediums. For instance, CNBC features almost exclusively interviews with large fund managers and important analysts. Filtering down to individual investors, CNBC further delineates the information and the system of knowledge by which other investors make judgements.

The squawk box is another device through which large institutional brokerage firms connect their retail and institutional brokers with corporate headquarters. Broadcasting continually throughout the day, squawk boxes relay daily interpretations of world events, top analyst's opinions on foreign investments, and information on other firms' activities – including the grading of country funds and changes in their recommended weightings of countries.

Market phenomenon and the homogenization of preferences

Herding, cascading, and lemming behavior

The fourth level of coordination lies within the nature of the financial markets themselves. This level is the degree to which investors will pay attention to what other investors are doing, or more importantly, might do. For instance, many investors tend to follow the leads set by other institutional investors or respected analysts in the field. It is implicit in the nature of stocks and bonds that a purchase is not a good investment if others do not at the time, or eventually, perceive it as a good investment as well. In addition, the need to minimize risk in a portfolio invites a natural tendency to follow convention. In essence, this phenomenon, referred to as herding, is a departure from the EMH discussed earlier.

This propensity to follow is confirmed by Ivo Welch, Sushil Bikhchandani and David Hirschleifer.[14] They find that when investors learn that their peers are investing in something, they tend to follow, even if their own judgment runs contrary (Pennar, 1995: 85). An 'informational cascade' is created when more and more investors join the growing bandwagon of opinion. These cascades often begin 'when just a few people decide to change course' (Pennar: 85). The Dow indicates the options market did anticipate a sharp decline in the market just before the 1987 crash (Pennar: 85). In addition, when the dollar surged in 1984–85 despite growing trade and budget deficits, the one-month forward indicators still predicted strength while the six-month indicators anticipated decline (Pennar: 85). This latter phenomenon highlights another finding of investment psychologists, 'that the most important factor influencing investor behavior is the recent past – recent news, recent earnings or, for that matter, recent trends in the markets' (Pennar: 84).

The reasons for herding – lack of information, cost of information, reputation of other investors, risk aversion, and information cascades – all play a part in the distortion of the emerging financial markets. In the emerging markets, where risks are greater and information scarcer, it is not surprising that emerging markets investors are often accused of lemming-like behavior. In a symbiotic relationship, many investors fall in line behind the beliefs of a few very large investors. Rob Johnson, a former portfolio manager for George Soros's Quantum Fund, depicts the lemming mentality among currency traders:

> Well, there is a very rational process going on in the financial markets. It goes kind of like this, 'I know I'm not that smart. But I know Soros is. So I'll watch what he's doing, and I'll go along for the ride' (Johnson, 1999).

This tendency to follow others comes in many varieties with varying consequences. In the case of bond traders, for instance, one can feign interest in a particular issue, say a Brazilian Brady bond, by buying noticeable amounts over a computer screen. Other bond traders can see this activity and may follow suit simply because they think someone knows something that they don't. Of course, this could be the case, or the trader could be trying to up the price so that she can unload a greater amount at a higher price. Apparently, this strategy is not uncommon among Brady and other bond traders.[15]

Following another firm's lead on investments is also common in less popular investment locations. For instance, when Botswana launched an issue of a local brewing company, Sechaba Investment Trust Company in 1996, very little buying of the US$20 million worth of shares occurred in the first two weeks of the sale. However, when a large well-known emerging market mutual fund purchased US$2 million worth, others followed suit. Andrew Ashton, analyst

for Stockbrokers Botswana Ltd., commenting on the ease of selling
the brewery company after this sale, suggested 'Once you have one
of them, the rest follow. It's like that all over the world' (Daley,
1996: A4).

Another instance where lemming-like behavior can be observed in
the emerging markets is in Mexico's peso devaluation in 1994.
Although domestic investors in Mexico were among the first to pull
their investments out of Mexico prior to the devaluation, the problems started much earlier as a speculative bubble developed as Mexico
became the darling of foreign investors. A similar argument could be
made for the heavy investing in Asia shortly before its emerging
stock markets crashed in 1997. Despite warnings that currencies
were in danger and the risks in Mexico and Asia had accelerated,
investors continued to follow each other into the bubble. In such
cases, fear of missing the boat outweighs the fear of losing the shirt.
Moreover, if everyone is losing, it is more acceptable to lose than if
others are winning and you are losing.

The investor tendency to follow one another buttresses the
already powerful positions held by the lead managers. Moreover, if
this pervasive psychological phenomenon is combined with the
close communications networks between firms, investor actions
become even more cohesive. This uniformity of both action and
opinion – combined with the additional fears associated with
emerging market risk and the relative scarcity of good information –
further congeals a pack mentality.

Institutions: private non-governmental associations (NGOs) and multinational organizations

The fifth level of coordination takes place in the organizations and
institutions working to help realize the goals of these institutional
investors. Both governmental and non-governmental entities are
instrumental in acting as third parties to organize and implement
policies favorable to investor-driven capitalism. This type of coordination is usually overt and can either take the form of associations
of international investors or multinational institutions like the
World Trade Organization or the IMF. The actions on this level can
consist of influencing domestic and foreign policy; developing and
maintaining the international finance regime; and procuring favorable outcomes from multilateral institutions like the IMF and World

Bank. David Mulford, CS Boston, comments on the need for such coordination as he states:

> you [investor] need the personal relationships, the contacts, the exchange of information and the agreement on which data to share: You have to have an ongoing process of coordination under way, however frustrating or difficult, because one of these times, you might actually be able to achieve something tangible when you need to in a crisis. It is the process that is important.[16]

The tripartite alliance of institutional investors, private associations, and government agencies forms a powerful unity of opinion and force within global finance.

The involvement of these organizations in creating developing countries' financial infrastrucutures, while arguably politically and economically beneficial in part, can also have possible consequences for democracy. In an insightful essay, Tony Porter outlines three ways in which transnational organizations can encroach upon democracy. First, as decision-making moves away from state structures to international ones, democratic deliberation becomes less likely. Secondly, treating policy issues with public consequences as technical, and therefore not appropriately subject to popular scrutiny, diminishes the likelihood of citizen participation. Thirdly, as private transnational associations increase their activity in assisting developing countries form the necessary legal and regulatory frameworks investors seek, public policy runs the risk of becoming privately run (Porter, 1999: 106). The following examples of private associations and multilateral institutions highlight some of the above phenomena.

Private associations

The many organizations representing the interests of large investors range considerably in size and scope. Some have specifically formed to address issues in the emerging markets and others have spawned committees dedicated to promoting the interests of their members in emerging market investing. In most cases, direct or indirect influence over policy directions in developing countries is an inherent, and often explicit, goal. As aforementioned, as private international organizations increasingly seek to influence policy in developing countries, the scope of democracy is potentially diminished as public matters fall under the purview of an elite group of financial moguls. Three important associations which work in concert to promote the interests of emerging markets trading are highlighted, the Emerging Markets Trading Association, the Council of Institutional Investors, and the Institute of International Finance.

The New York-based Emerging Markets Trading Association states as its primary goal, 'to promote the orderly development of a fair, efficient and transparent trading market for Emerging Markets instruments'.[17] In addition, they analyse local law issues, collect data, lobby, and perform risk analysis for their members. Focusing primarily on secondary markets such as Brady bond trading, they see their role as 'making the world safe for capitalism'.[18] They state: 'If there are differences in operations [between countries] then there are efforts to bring about conformity to our system.'[19] In other words, they try to recreate the US regulatory and legal structures that protect the interests of their members, almost exclusively institutional investors.

Another influential association is the Washington DC-based Council of Institutional Investors. With a budget of over US$1 million and 105 members, this organization's goal is to 'encourage pension fund trustees to take an active role in assuring that corporate actions are not taken at the expense of shareholders.'[20] The Council acts as a lobbying arm for large institutional investors as well, recommending policy positions on state and federal regulatory and legislative matters. They also circulate a monthly newsletter, provide investment information to members, assist members to act together on certain investments, and hold two conferences per year. Their function as a clearinghouse and mouthpiece for members further concentrates the goals of institutional investors. The following list of some of their activities in 1998 provides an idea of the scope and direction of the Council:

Excerpts from '1998 Highlights from the Council of Institutional Investors':[21]

- Successfully completed a massive overhaul of the Council policies on corporate governance, adding new policies covering a range of issues from director criteria to executive and director compensation.

- Facilitated communication between Council members on controversial governance proposals, including dual class stock proposal at Marriott.
- Initiated and financed the Supreme Court challenge by the Florida State Board of Administration and the California Public Employees' Retirement System of a lower court ruling dismissing their appeal of a settlement of derivative suit against Archer Daniels Midland. The funds sought and won Supreme Court review of the question of whether a shareholder who objects to the proposed settlement or dismissal of a derivative suit has the right to appeal an adverse decision.
- Prepared amicus brief along with counsel on the Council's behalf to the Supreme Court. Led major effort…to assemble other investors and interested parties to submit additional institutional investor amicus briefs…
- Facilitated and coordinated information flow to senators and congressmen working on the Securities Litigation Uniform Standards Act, especially the provision carving out an exemption for public funds from the act.
- Provided information to numerous press people on a nearly daily basis resulting in over 400 stories specifically crediting the Council and many more referencing individual Council members to who we forward press representatives.
- Identified pension funds that could be lead plaintiffs in various cases, provided them the necessary information, and coordinated their work with various law firms.

The Council's activities range from financing Supreme Court appeals for institutional investors to organizing press releases. Moreover, as will be discussed in Chapter 5, central in much of this work is the Council's efforts to increase investor activism.

The Institute of International Finance is another powerful organization of institutional investors. Composed of 185 of the largest commercial and investment banks, hedge funds, mutual finds, and portfolio managers, the Institute of International Finance (IIF) is one of the most important organizations for institutional investors in the world. Institutional investors benefit immensely from the Fund's country analyses and risk assessments. The IIF, founded in 1982 by an organizing committee comprised of 30 banks interested in resolving debt crisis problems, allows members to share information about debtors and collaborate on policy positions in regulatory matters (Porter, 1999: 107). Their three stated goals are:

1) ... to support members' risk management, asset allocation, and business development in the emerging markets.
2) ... to serve as a forum for engaging the private financial community in discussions with Finance Ministers, Central Bank Governors, the IMF, the World Bank, and other multilateral agencies designed to enhance private sector – public sector cooperation.
3) ... to provide a vehicle for exchanging views on global financial supervision issues and to advance the common views of its members with key regulatory authorities.

These goals were reflected in the Institute's response to the Asian financial crisis and the various solutions proposed to prevent future crises. Through a variety of press releases, conference participation, and meetings with government officials, the IIF strongly urged limiting any solutions to voluntary compliance by international investors. Calling themselves 'the organization that can most appropriately represent the views of the internationally active private sector financial institutions,' the IIF commands a powerful and uniform presence in the policy debates regarding the financial futures of emerging market countries.[22]

Multinational organizations

As the multilateral development banks significantly decreased their role in providing sovereign governments with needed capital beginning in the 1980s; these Bretton Woods institutions began to favor strategies that facilitated private institutional investors. A World Bank official notes 'Where we were activists at one time in the late '80's, we're now being pulled in all kinds of directions both in the financial markets and the business environment.'[23] In one financial journal, the dilemma faced by the multilateral agencies in the 1990s is characterized by the subtitle: 'The development banks are trying to figure out how to aid the private sector without getting in the way of Adam Smith's invisible hand' (Nameth, 1993: 19). Another prominent business journalist remarked 'The time has come for the Fund [the IMF] to develop a dialogue with the private financial community while preserving its confidential relations with its members' (Muehring, 1995: 41). In initiating programs aimed at working with the private sector, the multilateral institutions, it should be said, were also trying to preserve their own well-being as well as maintain their past objectives of assisting developing countries. This argument, that certain international institutions help large investors, is not intended to imply that developing countries are necessarily all worse off by this uniformity of interest. Indeed, many conditions imposed by the IMF and World Bank, and favored by investors, have helped developing countries cut inflation, corruption, and debt and have allowed for important capital inflows. The increasingly strong influence of institutional investor interests on multilateral bank policies and programs, has however, served to narrow the scope of political and economic choices available to developing countries. In addition, this comraderie reduces the likelihood of developing a counterweight to investor interests through these international organizations.

One way in which these institutions help investors is by providing an ideological division between the political and the economic. In other words, their bureaucratically defined goals are explicitly focused on 'economic' development, implying that somehow what is 'economic' is something other than what is political. This division helps alleviate any responsibility investors, seen as involved only 'economically', may have in disrupting the political. David Pion-Berlin points out one of the problems with this division:

> ...the doctrine of economic neutrality cannot stand up under closer scrutiny. Common sense tells us that if economics is the study of how society chooses to use scarce resources to produce and distribute commodities, then it is anything but neutral. Allocative decisions – who gets what, when, and how – have always been at the center of political life.

Pion-Berlin goes on to say that 'Economics as value-free science has often been used as a device to disguise the contentious nature of allocative decisions' (Pion-Berlin, 1989: 8). He cites international lending institutions as common users of economics as a mask for the political. The following statement from a World Bank president illustrates the point that the loans granted have strings attached and are not as apolitical as normally presented by lending officials:

> We ask a lot of questions and attach a lot of conditions to our loans. I need hardly say that we would never get away with this if we did not bend every effort to render the language of economics as morally antiseptic as the language the weather forecaster uses in giving tomorrow's prediction (Swedberg, 1986: 377).

In this statement, there is at least an implicit recognition that economics has political consequences. In today's explosion of free market liberalism, however, there is less institutional propensity to underestimate the negative political consequences associated with the expansion of liberal economic doctrine.

International institutions assist large investors in four primary ways. First, they help construct the international financial systems in emerging markets. The international financial system did not just happen. While the history of its construction, beginning even before Bretton Woods, is vital to understanding some of the processes of financial globalization occurring today, it is beyond the scope of this book. However, three more recent contributions to the building of emerging capital markets illustrate the role the IMF and World Bank have played in erecting elements of today's international financial regime. The IMF's structural adjustment programs beginning in the 1980s, the IFC's establishment of the first emerging markets fund in 1984, and the planning and implementation of the 'new' international financial architecture beginning in 1997, are examples of how the multilaterals have worked with large investors to construct and modify the system governing capital distribution to emerging markets. Secondly, multilateral lending institutions help investors by providing information and implementing international financial standards and codes in developing countries. Providing information through services like the IFC's Emerging Market Data Base, reduces investor costs. Standardization of data through services like IMF Special Data Dissemination, eases investor analysis and risk. Thirdly, multilaterals help monitor emerging markets' adherence to established financial market norms through loan conditionality, surveillance, and country reports. Fourthly, multilaterals can help maintain the system through crisis intervention and damage control that preserves the free capital market norms. Stepping in to lend to countries that have followed IMF or World Bank conditions and are in danger of economic crises, helps ensure continued participation and adherence to the established financial norms. The following section discusses some ways the aforementioned activities are performed by the World Bank, the IMF, and the OECD. Utilizing a variety of mechanisms, these institutions assist large investors by performing tasks like opening up new financial markets, providing information on investment opportunities, developing and implementing regulations protecting investor interests, and assisting investors invest through co-investing and insurance assistance. The following sections describe some of the IMF's, World Bank's, and OECD's specific programs and activities geared towards the above objectives.

The IMF

The IMF helped set the stage for increased private flows to developing countries and has increasingly recognized the importance of working with institutional investors to achieve its objectives. The IMF structural adjustment programs of the 1980s represent in many ways the beginning of this era's neoliberal consensus around economic development. Moreover, although the IMF can advocate market interventions to achieve its objectives, capital market liberalization in developing countries remains a central goal. Championing institutional investor interests, despite at times its social costs, is not coincidental. Increasingly beholden to the international financial markets, the IMF needs these investors if they are to have any hope of their economic stabilization agendas for countries in crisis to work. 'In a world with few controls on either capital or current accounts or on the huge swells of funds flowing across borders, leverage lies with the markets, not the Fund; that realization is shifting the concept of IMF surveillance to include the more active participation of the private markets' (Muehring, 1995: 40). Morris Goldstein, commenting on the relative power of the IMF and the emerging capital markets, states: 'Marshaling $5 billion is a big effort for the Fund, but is nothing to the other guys – the private institutional investors – who are moving the real money'

(Muehring, 1995: 40). The IMF, in essence, can no longer hope to achieve its economic objectives in countries without the tacit, and often explicit, approval of the private investment community. This has given large investors an inexpensive and loyal workforce that plans and implements many of the economic policies that benefit them.

The IMF assists private institutional investors through a variety of different programs and objectives, many of which are beyond the scope of this book. Some of the more prominent areas that facilitates the expansion of portfolio investor needs into developing countries will be addressed. The Enhanced Structural Adjustment Facility (ESAF), offering concessional medium-term loans to countries needing cash, typically makes funds available through contingent structural adjustment programs (SAPs) that often ultimately benefit large investors disproportionately. The New Arrangements to Borrow (NAB) and General Arrangements to Borrow (GAB), emergency credit lines available through the IMF that help avert, or lessen the effects of, a balance-of-payments crisis, also provide large investors with several significant benefits. Moreover, in addition the benefits attached to these loans, the IMF has developed significant working relationships with private investors through various initiatives. One result of these initiatives was the IMF Special Data Dissemination Standards (SDDS), a device that encourages uniformity of standards by which investors compare investment opportunities, easing their burden of data collection and comparison.

ESAF

The structural adjustment programs advanced by the ESAF benefit large investors by requiring loan recipients to open capital markets, privatize industries, and increase financial transparency. Since the Asian crisis, proposals have been made to expand the scope of the ESAF loan conditions to include data adequacy and transparency, financial legal frameworks, and corporate governance implementation.

The loan conditions benefit portfolio investors by paving the way for the entrance of portfolio capital through mandating capital controls easing, state-owned enterprises privatization (requiring the sale of shares), and financial statistics reporting.

NAB and GAB

The crisis prevention measures carried out by the IMF can have substantial, immediate benefits to private investors. Through the GAB, and now NAB, pre-emptive bailouts, like Brazil's in 1999, can allow foreign investors to be paid back, instead of losing their investment or renegotiating terms. In the case of Brazil, debt renegotiations were not demanded in return for the US$41.5 billion IMF loan. Many institutional investors, in fact, profited from the devaluation. Chase Manhattan, for instance, made '$150 million in January 1998, more than double its net income in Brazil' the preceding year, and JP Morgan and Citibank made huge profits as well (Romero, 1999). Banco Matrix, an investment bank, 'in January alone...quadrupled its earnings for all of 1998' (Romero, 1999). When used to repay debts to large investors and banks, however, these loans can also cause problems of moral hazard. Large investors become more confident of bailouts, and thus apportion more to those countries more likely to receive emergency relief. While in the long term, betting strongly on the likelihood of a bailout is ill-advised, as in the case of Long-Term Capital's highly leveraged bets on Russia, in the short-term, bailouts effectively diminish risk to investors. Moreover, bailouts also can present important political opportunities for the implementation of politically unpopular intensified austerity measures, often in the form of social spending cuts and/or wage repression.[24] This implementation and/or intensification of austerity measures creates buying opportunities for investors.[25] In addition, as in the case of structural adjustments programs, conditionalities like privatization can also be attached to bailout money. Crises intervention can enhance the opportunity for the IMF to win economic reform concessions from the country in crisis. These concessions most frequently intensify previous structural adjustment measures whose success relies heavily on attracting foreign investments. Thus, the benefits to institutional investors can often be immediate and greater.[26] For instance, his February 1999 visit to Brazil to negotiate the US$41.5 billion loan package, IMF Deputy Director, Stanley Fischer, urged President Cardoso to privatize the state oil company, Petroleo Brasileiro (Petrobras) and the state bank, Banco de Brasil.

The IMF loan packages offered to countries with a pending or current balance-of-payments crisis also boost domestic stock prices. The announcement of such loans raises the recipient country's stock market index, thereby raising the profits of shareholders, which are usually wealthy segments of the domestic population and foreign investors. The *Middle East Economic Digest* reports, 'the Istanbul stock exchange 100-share index ... as a seven-day bear-run was reversed on 30 June by a surge of optimism that the IMF was close to delivering a financial support package' (1999: 28). The cause for this optimism was not only that the loan package would help Turkey meet some of its short-term debt obligations, but also the conditions attached to the loan would open up trade and the capital markets further. While market optimism can be relatively short-lived, as in the cases of the Asian bailouts, the conditions attached to these loans often provide these more significant longer-term benefits to investors. In addition, although debt re-negotiation is never the optimal strategy for investors, it can be a better alternative than default. The IMF and World Bank have been instrumental in working with private investors to restructure debt obligations. Current negotiations are underway to facilitate the orderly restructuring of debt obligations for countries in crisis.

Private sector initiatives

Pressure has been increasing for the IMF to adopt proposals that would make the IMF a more explicit arm of private institutional investors. In 1995, Charles Dallara, managing director at the International Finance Corporation, stated 'The time has come for the Fund to develop a dialogue with the private financial community while preserving its confidential relations with its members' (Muehring, 1995: 41). Again in 1995, Arminio Fraga, one-time managing director of the Soros Fund Management and now Brazil's Central Bank President, recommends that the IMF become a clearinghouse for macroeconomic data, or a 'world auditor of macroeconomics' (Muehring, 1995: 40). This would enable private investors to obtain more reliable and cheaper information. Another suggestion was that the IMF meet formally on a regular basis with the IIF and its 185 members which include the largest institutional investors. In general, large investors called for the IMF to assist them in data collection and standardization, and to work more closely with them in structuring the international financial markets.

In April 1996, the IMF responded to the suggestions made by the investment community and created the Special Data Dissemination

Standard. Citing the lack of transparency as a factor in the Mexican financial crisis in 1994, the IMF and other international institutions focused on increasing the quantity and quality of economic information available for investors.[27] Obtaining reliable information with which to compare investment opportunities in the emerging markets has been a central problem for investors. Making IMF member countries provide comprehensive and standardized macroeconomic statistics makes significant progress towards solving this dilemma. In addition to mandating these new standards of data dissemination, the IMF expanded the scope of member surveillance to include financial system and capital account issues.

Following the Asian crisis, the IMF renewed its attempt to work more closely with the private sector. In April 1998, the IMF Executive Board tried initiating new ways to involve the private sector in crisis prevention. Since this meeting, many IMF reports and policy proposals have emphasized the need to work with investors to avert and/or resolve financial meltdowns. While the success of the IMF, in conjunction with the Group of Seven (G-7), in making investors bear some responsibility in resolving a crisis remains to be seen, indications suggest that at least a few of their key ideas are on shaky ground. The influence of private investors on the IMF appears by following the IMF's attempt to implement one of its main objectives in resolving an economic crisis – restructuring bond contracts held by private investors.

In press conferences hosted, and reports issued, by the IIF, a consortium of institutional investors vehemently opposed measures proposed by the G-7 countries and the IMF to restructure poor nations' debt. Large investment banks in particular were angered by proposals that would require banks and bondholders to ease the terms of loan contracts for countries the IMF and G-7 are trying to help reduce debt obligations. They were also aggravated by additional clauses that would require them to extend short-term trade-finance loans automatically for countries needing IMF help and restrict their right to sue governments for loan defaults. In addition, the IMF attempt to formalize a lending policy to countries in default to commercial banks was unpopular among lending institutions.

Immediately following these policy recommendations, institutional investors issued warnings to the G-7 and the IMF that these proposals could endanger the much-needed capital flows to the regions they were trying to assist. William Rhodes, Vice Chairman of Citigroup announced at the press conference 'Mandatory clauses resolving loan and bond claims could stymie the flow of capital to emerging markets' (Kraus, 1999: 1). Josef Ackermann, on the Deutsche Bank AG board, joined Rhodes in warning that 'the proposals could prove counterproductive just as Asian and Latin American emerging market countries were beginning to regain access to international capital markets after being nearly cut off last year.' (Kraus, 1999: 1)

In the April 1999 press conference that immediately followed an IIF attack on the G-7/IMF debt contract clause, the IMF appears to back away from the appearance of wanting to mandate any involvement from the private sector. In the following transcript, for instance, the voluntary nature of proposed future debt restructurings is emphasized. Moreover, the IMF highlights its role as a collaborator and aide to investment firms as they deal with creditor debt and the possibility of default. Jack Boorman, Director of the IMF Policy Development and Review, responds to a question posed by Bloomberg's Mr Pelosky, addressing the displeasure of the IIF with the IMF staff report:

> Mr. Pelofsky: (Bloomberg) ... A couple of days ago the IIF actually put out a report and a letter to the IMF and the international community calling for the IMF not to push some of these very ideas that are included here [within the IMF staff report], such as bond contract amendments. I'm wondering what kind of response you have to that and how you see overcoming that difficulty or that displeasure from the private sector.

> Mr. Boorman: ... two things. One is we're not working towards a series of rules. We're working towards a series of principles that you can work from on a case-by-case basis. ... What we're looking for is a collaborative way of getting the debtor and creditors together in that extreme kind of situation under a system that would allow the bond holders as a group to solve what's called the collective action problem, to come down as a group to look at the situation of the country and to come to conclusions about what's necessary to help see the country ... (Boorman, 1999: 5).

The likelihood of including clauses in bond contracts that mandate debtor participation in renegotiations does not look good.

The World Bank

The World Bank and some of its components have also made the jobs of international money managers easier and, in many ways, their activities more cohesive. While the World Bank has divisions that do not directly pertain to investor interests, several parts of the bank serve the interests of private investors. In particular, the World Bank president, the IFC, the Treasury Group, and some particular initiatives provide incentives and reduce obstacles for institutional portfolio investments in developing countries.

The World Bank recognizes its changing role as private capital flows to developing countries have increased, and multilateral institution funding is cut or suspended by conservative members of Congress. The appointment of James Wolfenson, World Bank president since 1995, reflects these trends. Wolfenson, a veteran of Wall Street, has prioritized World Bank adaptation to the growth of private sector funding:

> The environment in which we operate has vastly changed in the last 10 years. The reason you have to focus people on change – in the last 10 years, the role of the multilateral and overseas development assistance has been reduced from $60 billion a year to roughly $40 billion a year. During that same period of time, private sector investing in the developing world has gone from $30 billion to $260 billion. What that says about this institution is that we better work more closely with the private sector. The private sector is now the financial, and in some sense, the technological engine of growth in many countries. And what you need to do is tap into that entrepreneurial activity and reconceive our own development plan within the context of what we do in partnership with the private sector. – Wolfenson (McTague, 1998: 28).

Wolfenson is well positioned to work in partnership with the private sector. After obtaining a MBA from Harvard, he became an investment banker in Europe. He then went on to Wall Street to work for one of the largest institutional investment firms at the time, Salomon Brothers. After leaving Salomon, Wolfenson began his own investment firm and built an empire worth more than US$100 million. Now, as *Barron's* reports, Wolfenson is 'attempting to bring

Wall Street creativity to the World Bank' (McTague, 1998: 27). The appointment of Wolfenson to the World Bank is indicative of the trends taking place in the bank's policies and approaches to development. Although its primary mandate includes a larger commitment to social issues than the IMF, the World Bank is playing a greater role in the establishment of financial market norms in developing countries.

IFC

Much of the World Bank's work in linking developing countries with private financiers occurs within the IFC, a division of the World Bank Group that is owned by 170 member countries. The IFC's role in creating, promoting, and maintaining portfolio flows into developing countries is a profoundly influential one.

Because of the status of the IFC as a not-for-profit organization and its ability to create one of the most extensive databases for emerging market information, it has become an important informational resource for large investors. The information it collects, however, is often costly, frequently allowing only larger firms access to its services. This cost-prohibitive practice promotes an exclusivity of information on the emerging markets, thus potentially narrowing the number of market participants and diminishing the extra liquidity needed to diminish the potential influence of large investors.

The IFC also limits the number of countries it covers, thereby reducing the likelihood of investors gaining important information about newer markets and countries with smaller market capitalization. As was previously addressed in the compilation of the IFC index of emerging market countries, the IFC has the potential to sway the markets with its ability to include or exclude, or underweight or overweight countries.

International Securities Group

The International Securities Group (ISG), a section of the IFC explicitly established 'in response to ... the increasing interests of international investors in emerging markets', acts a conduit between firms in need of financing in developing countries and institutional investors (IFC, 1999: 1). Their activities assist private investment firms in a variety of ways. First, they help identify firms that would like to go public – a task that normally costs investment firms a great deal of money in research and sales. The ISG brings these potential clients to commercial banks and investment firms with which it has established relationships. In essence, the ISG provides free marketing and public relations by increasing the visibility and credibility of the institutional investors with which they work.

Once an appropriate financing vehicle is established, the ISG then contributes a number of services benefiting the investment partner. They provide underwriting and placement services to complement private services. This includes joint-lead managing of bond issues, Initial Public Offerings (IPOs), and mutual funds. After placement, they continue support by facilitating communications between firms and investors, 'providing feedback from our investor base' (IFC, 1999b: 1). They are indeed, responsible for 'the concept of emerging markets investments through the sponsorship, structuring, underwriting, and placement of country funds' (IFC, 1999c: 1). They also ensure clients that they 'place securities exclusively with major international institutional investors,' confining the placement of emerging market stocks to the same large, well-established, mostly Western-based, securities firms. For instance, of the last 31 joint-lead managed transactions handled by the IFC, 15 were handled by US firms and 12 handled by European firms. Three firms, Merrill Lynch, Morgan Stanley, and SBC Warburg, were awarded 11, or over 30 per cent, of these deals. The IFC may also choose to invest for their own account, again helping the institutional investors make the initial offering successful.

The Treasury Group, part of the World Bank that is responsible for raising funds through the sale of debt and investing profits and the bank's pension fund, is also a very influential force in global finance. Known for its level of sophistication in bond offerings, the World Bank is considered a role model in the way it reduces financing costs in raising debt.[28] Because of its status in global finance, as well as its activities as a money manager, developing countries look to the World Bank for guidance on their financial infrastructures and policies. Recreating a financial infrastructure in the image of industrialized countries eases administrative and legal obstacles Western investors may face in dealing with a system unlike their own. As an adviser to emerging market countries, the World Bank 'will share its risk-management systems and its asset-allocation and trading models with its emerging market 'customers.' Many EMCs also get advice on how to privatize their social-security systems' (Doherty, 1998: 30). This advice from the Treasury Group can serve to broaden the number of financial instruments used by investors from emerging markets as well as increase the size of their market capitalization, both of which can help foreign investors. Recommending the use of derivatives for hedging purposes, for instance, may send emerging market customers to the already established hedge funds. In addition, increasing market capitalization through the privatization of social-security systems can also have a positive impact on the price of foreign-held stocks.

World Bank initiatives and objectives

In addition to the departmental activities of the IFC and the Treasury Group, the World Bank promotes the interests of private investors through a series of initiatives and objectives that are implemented by various parts of the Bank. The following section discusses some of the more important World Bank activities that coincide with large investor concerns and help configure the legal, political, and economic frameworks attractive to portfolio financiers.

Global corporate governance forum

The World Bank has recently added another means by which they will try to assist private investors – the Global Corporate Governance Forum. Corporate governance, or the regulations that outline corporate power structures, defines the relationships between management, board of directors, and shareholders and how they are to set, implement, and monitor corporate objectives. This initiative officially began on 21 June, 1999, when President Wolfensohn and OECD Secretary-General Don Johnston signed a memorandum of understanding creating a public–private partnership dedicated to expanding Western-style corporate governance laws into developing countries. In the wake of the Asian crisis, international agencies, private organizations, and corporations came together to form this entity to advocate and help implement corporate standards and laws for developing countries. These new regulations would improve investor access to corporate information, empower corporate boards, and expand shareholder rights. All of these provisions would serve the interests of private investors. In particular, if shareholder rights expanded enough to match US shareholder rights, corporate policies in developing countries that govern levels of employment, wages, and plant closings, would come increasingly under the jurisdiction of institutional investment firms. This initiative, located in the World Bank's Washington headquarters, could 'emerge as part of World Bank loan programs'.[29]

Privatization initiatives

Privatization is an essential component to the expansion of capital markets in emerging market countries. Often the largest companies on an emerging market stock exchange are those that were previously state-owned enterprises. Thus, privatization has been central to the expansion of emerging stock markets and the increased ownership of large investors. Privatizing, with costs and benefits to developing countries, offers large investment firms the opportunity for substantial profits through fees for managing IPOs, commissions for subsequent transactions on the stocks, and profit if owned shares increase in value. For instance, a 1992 World Bank report estimated that the sale of Mexico's national telephone company, Telmex, cost consumers 92 million pesos (US$33 billion) while foreign investors made 67 trillion pesos, about 90 per cent of the net benefits from the sale (Hansen-Kuhn, 1997: 2). Privatizing also means that investors, predominantly large and Western, will increasingly have control over the vital industries in developing countries.

The World Bank, like the IMF, has been instrumental in encouraging privatization in developing countries. As aforementioned, the recommendation for developing countries to privatize their state-owned enterprises (SOEs) directly benefits large investors. Similar to the IMF, privatization is often attached as a conditionality of a loan package, and has been important in the World Bank's promotion of economic liberalization. For instance, in May 1998, a US$530 million balance of payments support package for Zambia was withheld by the World Bank until Zambia Consolidated Copper Mines was completely privatized (Kunda, 1999: 2). In Pakistan, the World Bank recently advised the sale of nationalized banks to help repay US$32 billion in foreign debt. Moreover, in this case, the World Bank reported that not only should the sale be the 'primordial objective, under which other objectives would subsume,' but also, in order to help achieve the objective, 'participation by reputable international banks would need to be encouraged' (Bokhari, 1999: 3). In other words, the World Bank was also trying to stipulate the participation of larger and more established banks in the process, thus reinforcing the participation of large investors in the privatization process. With the increasing enhancement to corporate governance regulations and, hence shareholder rights, large investors will continue to garner substantial power within developing countries' largest corporations. Thus, the IMF and World Bank will effectively increase the power of investors in developing countries through the continued enforcement of privatization and likely enhancement of shareholder rights.

Another area in which the Bank supports private portfolio investors, is through investment guarantees, or insurance on investments. Conducted through the Multilateral Investment Guarantee Agency (MIGA), this insurance program offers investors a means to reduce their risks of investing in developing countries. Although the investments insured are labeled 'FDI' rather than equity investments, as Chapter 1 pointed out, this distinction is now blurred by the securitization of corporate and project loans. Thus, MIGA is very often helping to protect equity investments. For instance, in the largest contract ever issued by MIGA, a guarantee to cover an investment for the expansion of Banque Nationale Paris in Russia, a 'shareholder' loan was given US$90 million in coverage.[30] On a smaller scale, MIGA issued US$1.8 million in coverage for a US$2 million equity investment in Zambia (MIGA, 1999). In February 1999, MIGA also expanded the amount of political risk insurance it offers investors, from a $50 million project limit to $110 million (MIGA, 1999). MIGA also launched in June 1998, a service for investors to obtain information on privatizations taking place in developing countries. Providing investors with a database of companies and assets for sale, links to government and private organizations dedicated to helping them, and a privatization law library, this web site can greatly reduce the costs of investing. As one MIGA official states: 'We are pleased to build upon the success of IPAnet [Investment Promotion Network] by launching this important new resource for the benefit of the international investment community...' (MIGA, 1999).

The World Bank, through MIGA, also hosts a web site called 'FundLine' that facilitates investments in Eastern Europe and the Former Soviet Union. This site provides investors with information about who is investing in what countries, which firms manage funds in which countries, the types of industries funds are invested in, and the types of investments that are available. Fundline also benefits fund managers and investment firms by advertising their fund for prospective investors as well as companies seeking investments and investment services. For instance, firms can search the site looking for particular funds interested in a particular industry. Tobacco related firms, for example, can identify funds interested in investing in tobacco. In essence, Fundline provides a convenient, World Bank-endorsed, and free means in which fund managers can express their preferences in industries and financing instruments.

Revolving door

Another phenomenon that reinforces the linkages and unifies the goals of the World Bank and IMF with institutional investors is the constant exchange, both temporary and permanent, of staff between these multilaterals and the large financial firms. Known as the 'revolving door,' this practice occurs on both formal and informal levels. On the formal level, for instance, the World Bank encourages staff exchanges through the official channel of its Staff Exchange Program. This program has developed partnerships with a variety of institutional investment firms, including Chase Manhattan, Deutsche Bank, Dresdner Bank, JP Morgan, and Sanwa Bank.

'Revolving door' is a term often used to describe the bureaucratic-interest group linkages in which a government employee leaves a government post for the private sector and becomes an advisor/lobbyist to their old government agency. The World Bank and large investment firms also share this practice. The World Bank is fertile ground for the recruitment of money managers by private institutional investors and, conversely, the World Bank draws frequently from large investment firms for its staff. Many top managers at the Bank have already had substantial careers as institutional investors. For instance, the Executive Vice President of the IFC, Peter Woicke, was Chairman at JP Morgan before joining the World Bank Group. Peter Cook, a recently appointed director of the IFC's Asia Department, worked at Morgan Stanley for 27 years prior to this position. Table 4.2 shows some other staff exchanges occurring within the World Bank.

Table 4.2 Institutional investor affiliations of World Bank and IMF employees

Name	Multilateral bank/government affiliations	Private sector affiliations
Charles Dallara	Managing Director, IFC	Managing Director, Institute of International Finance
Thomas Dawson	Director, IMF External Relations (former IMF Executeve Director)	Director, Financial Institutions Group, Merrill Lynch
Edward Kane	Consultant for World Bank, Congress Budget Office	Consultant for American Bankers Association
Gerard Caprio	Lead Economist, World Bank Development Research Group	Vice president, JP Morgan
Peter Cook	Director, Asia Department, IFC	Various positions for 27 years, Morgan Stanley
Peter Woicke	Executive Vice President, IFC	Chairman, JP Morgan Securities Asia
Richard Frank	Managing Director, World Bank	Managing Partner, Darby Overseas Investments
Steven Schoenfeld	IFC, developed investment vehicle based on IFC indexes	Investment strategist, Barclays Global Investors' Emerging Strategies

In a direct incident of the revolving door, Jamshid Ehshani, once an employee of the Treasury Group, left for Citibank and began working as a consultant to the World Bank on bond offerings (Doherty, 1998: 30). These exchanges, and the revolving door practice, reinforce the linkages between private sector and multilateral institutions like the World Bank.

OECD and the Multilateral Agreement on Investment

Investors are also assisted by multilateral institutions through the creation and implementation of international treaties. A look at some of the OECD's work in the late 1990s provides an example of how international organizations focused on opening trade and finance, can exclude groups impacted by multinational agreements. For instance, the process of creating the Multilateral Agreement on Investment (MAI) had important ramifications for democratization in developing countries.

Although tabled in its present form, the Multilateral Agreement on Investment (MAI) provides a striking example of the increasingly collaborative and convenient relationships being established between institutional investors and international institutions. The provisions of the MAI also represent similar types of international guidelines in progress at the World Trade Organization and the IMF. Housed since 1995 at OECD headquarters in Paris, the MAI was being developed by transnational corporations and international trade bureaucrats from industrialized countries. Supported by the Clinton administration, the MAI was slated to come up for congressional debate in October 1998. Essentially, the MAI is an international agreement that sought to reduce regulatory and other barriers to international corporate investors. The text of the agreement included some of the following provisions:

- The treaty would protect large corporate investments from 'revolution, states of emergency or any other similar events'. Under this provision, events such as strikes, boycotts, and protests could provide foreign investors with the right to demand compensation for any losses that occurred due these types of 'strife' (Anderson, 1998: 6).
- The treaty would abolish 'performance requirements' of corporations. Lori Wallach, legal expert on the MAI, speculated that this

would effectively 'abolish the very policy tools that countries need more than ever to counter currency attacks and stabilize national stock markets' (Anderson, 1998: 6).

● The treaty would also undermine developing countries' ability to regulate capital flows, thus preventing 'countries from imposing conditions on portfolio investment, such as 'speed bumps' which are requirements that investors hold onto financial instruments for a certain length of time' (Anderson, 1998: 6). Thus, entry and exit requirements would be eliminated, greatly reducing the sovereignty and capacity of developing countries to protect themselves from speculative traders.

● The MAI would prohibit signatory governments to sanction nations for human rights violations, environmental and labor practices.[31]

The implications of this type of treaty for democracy are significant in at least five ways. First, the process by which this treaty and others like it have been drafted excludes the vast majority of people who will be affected by their adoption. Secondly, the agreement would severely curtail voices of dissent against corporate practices, corruption, and authoritarian governments by encouraging repression through holding recipients of foreign investment liable for various forms of political instability perceived disruptive to corporate profits. Thirdly, this type of agreement constrains those international organizations and measures aimed at sanctioning anti-democratic practices. For instance, under the MAI no-sanctions provision, 'the worldwide sanctions that eventually brought down South Africa's apartheid regime would have been prohibited' (Anderson, 1998: 5). Fourthly, insofar as a healthy environment is part of peoples' rights in a well-functioning democracy, the MAI would help dismantle the ability of governments to establish and maintain safeguards against corporate disregard for the environment. Environmentalists like Friends of Earth President Brent Blackwelder goes so far as to say that 'the MAI would be a dagger through the heart of democracy' (Anderson, 1998: 3). Fifthly, the MAI's provision for dispute resolution essentially excludes the average citizen entirely. An individual cannot appeal to the international tribunal, nor is there any public transparency or public participation requirements. The contents of the MAI and the process of its conception reflect the limited scope of the OECD agenda as it seeks to maintain and buttress the strength of global financiers and large corporations. Although the MAI has been set aside for now, it represents a trend occurring in many international institutions in which the interests of large corporations are of foremost concern.

Conclusions: systemic cohesion and neoliberal adhesion

Coordination of thought and action the world of global finance is evident as one observes the many levels of interaction that take place on ideological, corporate, communicative, institutional, and market levels. Although only composing a tiny fraction of the world's population, the world's large financiers control the majority of the world's financial resources. As Chapter 2 suggested, those controlling emerging market capital flows represent an even smaller portion of this already small number of people charged with the task of managing the world's money. This chapter has outlined the ways in which this small world is able to create and maintain systemic norms, beliefs, and practices that ultimately preserve a consensus beneficial to those within. Chapter 5 will look at those individuals who have defended the adhesion to neoliberalism by utilizing capital resources to influence the direction of policies in developing countries.

5
Expression of Preferences: Front-running, Investor Activism, and Other Market Influences

The last chapter focused on the systemic characteristics of international financial markets that help support the idea that these markets are not the efficient, abstract mechanisms neoliberalism proposes, but fairly organized networks of communication and cooperation between large investors. The potential power of these investors lies not only in the large amounts of capital they control as individual firms but also in the ideological norms and cooperative practices that unify their preferences to developing countries. This chapter, however, addresses the power individual institutional investors can and do wield over emerging market countries. It is divided into three sections. The first section discusses the practices utilized by investors to influence the direction of particular stocks and markets, and explores the increased potential for market manipulation, in particular front-running. The second section considers the presence of investor activism, or corporate governance, in the emerging markets and looks at some cases in which large investors attempted to change policy outcomes. The third section provides a brief glimpse at evidence that belies the presence of the power investors have over policy in emerging market countries.

Front-running

As investors accrue more power to sway markets in the as-yet relatively unregulated and illiquid emerging markets, it is increasingly likely investors will be able to exert influence over smaller investors and developing country corporations and government officials. This is particularly true in those countries relying most on equity capital. This section discusses the potentially fertile ground emerging markets have for market-manipulating activities such as front-running.[1]

When investing, investors want to foresee not only increasing popularity of a country or particular stock, but also want to persuade others to invest as they did. In addition, if knowledge of an impending large investment is available, investors with this inside information can invest before the news hits the streets and drives the price up. The same is true of course for an impending sell order. This activity, where one trades for their own benefit before executing a large order, is known as front-running. Although illegal in most securities markets, this activity often goes undetected and unreported. One of the reasons is that in the domestic US market, information has become more widely available and there are many more traders in the markets. Therefore, it is much harder, according to economist Ivo Welch, to front-run these days in the developed financial markets.[2] However, in the emerging markets, there are several elements that can make front-running easier and more effective. It is very likely that large investors are more able to influence the emerging markets because of the scarcity of information, lower numbers of large investors, illiquidity in the markets, and lack of regulations safeguarding against front-running. One of the most common opportunities to front-run is in the endless amount of surveys published in which financial analysts from large institutions are polled on their portfolio holdings, predictions for good investments, and risks to avoid. Front-running can occur, for instance, when an investor comments on the ill-health of a country while purchasing shares in it or, conversely, sells shares while commenting on the benefits of a country or corporation. Another example is when a broker gets an order from a large institutional investor and buys or sells for their own account, possibly driving the price of the stock up or down to the client's disadvantage. Detection of front-running, however, is very difficult unless one is able to obtain proprietary information on holdings on a day-to-day basis. The Securities and Exchange Commission (SEC) regularly monitors large US investors for front-running but emerging market holdings fall under the purview of domestic regulatory agencies only if they are purchased through ADRs or other such domestically based investment vehicles. Detection and regulation of international capital flows is still in its relative infancy, leaving the door open for possible market manipulations such as front-running.

Front-running in emerging markets occurs on a fairly regular basis according to one trader. Clive Williams, a trader with LGT Asset Management PLC in London commented: 'You'd be amazed how often I'm told that Templeton or Fidelity is buying ... [brokers] use codes: They tell you "Bald Eagle" is buying, and you know it's Mobius.'[3] The occurrence of front-running in and of itself does not necessarily effect the politics in emerging market countries. However, its existence demonstrates the relative power one or two large investors can wield over an emerging stock market, and subsequently, over the country's potential status in the international financial markets.

Investor activism

The ascendancy of international investor power is perhaps best understood by first looking at the trends within US investor–corporate relations. Much has been written about the ascendancy of investor power over corporations in the US. Known as corporate governance, or investor activism, the exertion of power by large investors on corporate policy, top officers, and general strategy has received growing attention in the 1990s.

In 1992 the SEC changed one of its rules on investor communication and opened the door for investors to communicate behind closed doors about their mutual investments. Armed now with a lot more capital, and the ability to collaborate, institutional investors are capable of controlling even some of the largest US corporations. One of the most comprehensive looks at investor power in the US is Michael Useem's *Investor Capitalism*. Although Useem's work deals primarily with institutional investor activism in US corporations, it provides a useful representation of the structures, methods, and results of investor rule, and an important parallel between the US and emerging financial markets. Essentially, Useem argues that the enormous upsurge in the capital markets in the last ten years has been accompanied by a great increase in the power shareholders wield over corporations. The change in the concentration of assets,

or 'the crowding of equities into fewer hands', is the primary catalyst for this increase in power (Useem: 25). In 1965, 84 per cent of
corporate stock was held by individual investors and only 16 per
cent by institutions. By 1994, institutions controlled 46 per cent and
individuals ownership had dropped to 56 per cent (Useem: 25).
Fueled by the vast growth in pension funds, the new institutional
shareholders have formed a new political base.

Useem suggests that this phenomenon has ushered in a new era
of capitalism – investor capitalism. He argues that in the 1980s and
through the 1990s, large shareholders began to realize the extent of
their power and became more active in communicating their specific desires to corporations. By organizing with other investors to
realize their goals, institutional investors utilized various degrees of
persuasion, including threats to divest, to achieve their objectives.
Keeping in mind that these shareholders are often the same or
within the same corporation as those investing in emerging markets, it is easy to draw parallels between this US investor trend and
investor activism in the developing markets.

What is the process of investor activism? Why would a large
investor choose to engage in the running of a corporation instead of
simply divesting? There are several reasons. First, large investors are
often simply too large to be choosy. If an institution already has an
excess of investable assets and its options are constrained by internal mandates and the availability of investable options, it is not so
easy to simply withdraw funds. The California State Teacher's
Retirement System's chief investment officer, in control of over
US$46 billion in assets, states: 'The larger public pension funds can't
just walk away when companies aren't performing well. There'd be
no market. Everybody would be on one side of the trade' (Useem:
31). The chief investment officer at Calpers, responsible for US$68
billion, mentions the same constraint: 'We realized we don't have
the option of voting with our feet. The only course available is to
see [that] companies are effectively run' (Useem: 30). A pension
fund manager of College Retirement Equities Fund further under-
scores the point: 'Buying stock in a company is like buying a purple
house. If you don't like the color, you can sell the house or you can
paint it. ... We're doing a lot more painting.'[4]

A second reason it behooves large investors to do more than enter
and exit investments is that many Western-based companies have

been greatly overpriced, and new, less expensive ventures are in demand. The large investment companies have taken it upon themselves to mold new investment sites into more attractive prospects. In the emerging markets, this may include attempts to reshape the political landscape as well.

Similarities and differences between domestic and international investor activism

The goals of the domestic and international institutional investments are essentially the same. Rates of return, diversification, growth, and currency risk management are some of the primary aims of larger investors. When looking at a domestic corporation, an investor normally surveys its history of returns, dividend yield, growth, and price to earnings ratios. In addition, Useem outlines six areas of concern that investors have focused their energies when trying to influence the operations of US corporations. These are: (1) Shareholder voice inside the company; (2) Workforce size; (3) Redesign; (4) Company strategies; (5) Executive leadership and succession; and (6) Corporate governance (Useem: 138). When institutional investors look at an emerging market country or corporation, these areas or their counterparts are added to political and currency risk to assess potential profits. In other words, institutional investors will look not only at these concerns on the corporate level, but will also be concerned with similar issues on a country level.

The differences between an emerging market investment and a domestic investment are also worth noting. Emerging market investments are more cost-intensive because of the added costs of international travel, research, and communication. In addition, the numbers reported by a firm in an emerging market country are often compiled differently, not as comprehensive or accurate as domestic firms, and are often not subject to the same legal scrutiny. Visits to these firms are often vital to assess investment viability and communicate shareholder expectations. However, perhaps the most important difference is the added need for an investor to assess the social, political, and economic variables in an emerging market country. If one takes the aforementioned areas of investor concern as outlined by Useem and extrapolates them to a country level, one can get a picture of the areas of concern that investors can have within this additional level of scrutiny. Table 5.1 draws such parallels.

Table 5.1   Institutional investor concerns: domestic and emerging
markets

Domestic corporations	Emerging market countries
Shareholder voice	Foreign shareholder rights
Work size force	Labor controls
Redesign	Content of reform
Company strategies	Implementation of reforms
Executive leadership and	Ability of leaders and
succession	regime stability
Corporate governance	Influence over policy

When an institutional investor is looking into investing in a company within an emerging market, both the corporate and country
concerns come into play. The methods used to communicate the
preferences of these investors vary and Useem offers a list of some of
these. Stressing the importance of strengthening investor-corporate
relations, Useem advises institutional investors to have various tools
at their disposal to achieve the preferred outcomes in the aforementioned concerns. Calling it a new order of investment-management
relations, Useem provides an outline of the new norms that
'describe and prescribe much of the evolving thrust of investor–
company relations' (Useem: 274). The following six principles (in
italics) are extracted from Useem's list while the descriptions following pertain to investor relations with developing countries' governments, elites, and corporations, rather than with the US corporations
of Useem's focus.

1. *Press for performance*: If governments are not meeting the
expectations of the investment community, investors are not shy
about pressing for political restructuring at ministerial or higher
levels, implementation of particular reform measures, or select
strategies for currency handling, in particular devaluation.
Finance ministers and central bankers may be replaced if
investors don't respond well to them.

2. *Construct networks rather than markets or hierarchies*: Often
referred to as crony capitalism, the existence of contact networks
and the partnering of large corporate interests is commonplace in
developed and developing countries. Here, Useem is advocating
this explicitly as a business strategy necessary to compete in the
world of investor capitalism. In emerging markets, joining forces

with domestic elites is a basic tenet of the expansion of the finance industry.

3. *Disseminate information*: The information exchange between institutional investors and emerging market countries continues to grow but is still in its relative infancy. In particular, institutional investors, multilateral development agencies, and information technology firms are gathering data pertinent to investors. Lack of reliable information continues to be a problem for investors. In addition, the categorization process discussed in Chapter 4 has shaped the way in which this information is processed.

4. *Enhance mutual influence*: This tenet is a call to embrace the new relationship between investors and corporations. In the case of the emerging markets, this includes encouraging government leaders to be open to the ideas and strategies of large investors.

5. *Institutionalizing the relations:* Emerging market countries may formally set up ministries, bureaus, or organizations to deal with large investors. These new entities serve as clearinghouses of information as well as vehicles within the structures of government to express investor preferences. As these entities are usually located outside of elected offices, policies are often pushed through more quickly and easily than in the legislative branches. Russia's Federal Commission on Securities and Institute for Law-based Economy are two examples of government-sponsored, Western-funded organizations that were founded without parliamentary approval and that had profound effects on Russia's economic policies. These organizations were also full of US advisers linked strongly to, or participating in, institutional investments.[5]

6. *Contest the electoral process*: In the case of corporations, this can mean exercising shareholder rights to vote on corporate decisions, including company leadership, salaries, and voting rights. Shareholders of emerging market stocks, as in the Cukurova Electric case discussed later in this chapter, are trying to increase their voice in company matters through an expansion of voting rights. In many cases, emerging market country corporations have been family owned or government controlled and shareholder rights are slow in coming. In the case of emerging market countries, institutional investors could influence the national electoral process if capital withdrawal appears to be threatened if unfavorable election results are predicted.[6]

These six norms are examples of how the US investor-activism paradigm can be exported to developing countries. Each of these norms recognizes, extends, and reinforces the control institutional investors may have over corporate and governmental policies. Useem also points out that some corporations are more susceptible to shareholder power than others. For example, a corporation that has an excellent record of financial management, has consistently shown profits, and is rated by others as a low-risk investment, is more likely to be able to act independently of investor control. Corporations with shaky pasts, bad credit ratings, and a history of unpredictable returns would be more susceptible to investor control. Emerging market countries as a category are considered much more susceptible than many Western countries or corporations because of past credit. Poor debt records and consequently poor credit ratings put emerging market countries in a much higher risk category. Combined with the unproven stability of a newer stock market, higher rates of volatility, and higher political and economic risks, emerging markets rarely can afford the luxury of ignoring investor demands.

With the knowledge that developing countries are hungry for capital and rarely enjoy low risk categorization, emerging market institutional investors have not been strangers to investor activism. In fact, their leverage over their investments is arguably stronger than it would be domestically given the aforementioned susceptibility of emerging market companies and countries. Visits to potential investment sites and in-country analysts, often imperative because of the lack of sufficient financial data from companies, are perfect vehicles for communicating investor needs to both corporations and government officials. As the *Wall Street Journal* reports '[emerging market] fund managers are...wielding their vast resources to cudgel corporations and governments alike' (Hirsch, 1996: 1). The investment community recognizes this power as well. Morgan Stanley fund manager, Paul Ghaffari, sees the emerging market debt crises as a 'wake-up call' to emerging market countries warning 'that they have to follow the right policies' and 'If they slip up, they will pay' (Gasparino, 1996: C1). Statistics show that in a span of four years, investor's rights have expanded considerably. For instance, US institutions increased their votes in foreign proxies from 24 per cent in 1991 to 65 per cent in 1994 (*Corporate Board*, 1996). The following examples of specific encounters between institutional investors and emerging market governments reveal the new role institutional investors are assuming in their attempts to influence government policy through investor activism.

Joyce Cornell, managing US$400 million at Scudder, Stevens, and Clark, took a four-day trip to the Philippines and met with 'high-level officials in the Philippine Congress, the Department of Finance, and the Central Bank of the Philippines' (Hirsch, 1996). Cornell, utilizing her power to influence political outcomes that might lower risk and increase returns, 'throws her weight behind tax-reform legislation that may be enacted by year end, gets critical cues about the currency from central bankers, and pushes a top legislator to consider agricultural reforms' (Hirsch, 1996: 3). In a meeting with one government official, Cornell, met with the insinuation that she thinks of the Philippines as the 'flavor of the month', suggests threateningly to 'tell your president he will fall off the list if tax reform doesn't pass' (Hirsch, 1996: 3). Cornell, pleased with her meetings, decided to purchase 1.1 million shares of a company developing the first casino resort in the country.

Many fund managers acquire reputations for their style of activism. Jim Mellon, the head of Regent Pacific, a money management firm based in the Cayman Islands, has been called 'brash, aggressive' and 'belligerent' (Norton, 1996: 1). Known for their activism, Regent Pacific has bullied several corporations in developing countries into seeing things their way. For instance, a well-known example of Regent Pacific's activism is its efforts to break up the family conglomerate, Pioneer Industries in Hong Kong.

Mark Mobius, manager of over US$10 billion of Templeton's emerging market funds and arguably the most well-known emerging market expert, is another example of the growing activism in emerging market investors. In a 1996 interview, Mobius admits that as his assets have grown, he has taken a larger role in controlling his investments. He states: 'We used to be very passive at the beginning, and if we didn't like the company, we would sell it. That has been our stance up to now. Now we are voting actively, and I think you will see more and more institutions acting in concert' (Dow Jones and Company 18 November 1996: 2). Commenting on his support of Regent Pacific's aforementioned efforts to break up the family-owned Pioneer Industries, Mobius stated: 'You have a real clash of cultures, because many of these families have treated shareholders paternalistically,

[and] there is tremendous resistance to any shareholder activism. But those days are numbered. Shareholders have rights' (op. cit.). Incidences of Templeton's activism, while often aimed at corporate management, can also involve government officials. An example of this type of activism occurred when Mobius influenced the Turkish government's policy and actions regarding a Turkish electric company, Cukurova Electric. In this case, Templeton had invested a substantial amount in an electric company in the early 1990s. In 1993, a family-owned conglomerate, the Uzan group, purchased a block of shares, making them the majority shareholder with 37 per cent ownership (Mobius, 1996: 336). After this acquisition, and through subsequent stock purchases by Uzan which eventually increased their position to a 67 per cent ownership, the company stock began to deteriorate and Templeton began to question some of Uzan's management practices (336). Templeton's initial step was to begin taking an active role in the shareholder meetings. The procedure of registering shares in order to participate, however, turned out to be much more difficult than was anticipated. Because of some bureaucratic red tape, the FID of Turkey denied their initial request to register their shares and Templeton was in danger of missing the next meeting. To rectify the situation, Templeton contacted President Tansu Ciller to intervene on their behalf so they may vote at the next meeting. President Ciller's office 'pressured the head of the FID and our shares were registered and an entry card provided' (339).

Templeton was not able to sway the vote at the meeting as a minority shareholder voting against a majority. However, the steps taken to gain access into the corporation's governance are representative of the types of institutional activism on the increase in developing countries. Utilizing the executive office in Turkey did not pose a problem for such a large investor as Templeton.

Mobius is also not afraid to withhold funds if countries do not provide acceptable investment opportunities. In the summer of 1994, Mobius raised US$120 million for his Templeton Vietnam Opportunities Fund. By June 1995, he had not invested any of it yet in Vietnam. He defends his decision not to invest as he states (Balfour, 1995: 205):

> We haven't been able to find anything we like. We don't have to throw money at any project because it happens to come our way. [Shareholders] pay us to make money, not to invest.

Mobius, unable to find enough investment opportunities in Vietnam, invested elsewhere with the funds and was sued by unhappy investors (Mellow, 1998).

Vietnam represents an important phenomenon in which investors raised massive amounts of capital before there was a place to put it. Macroeconomic statistics indicated that Vietnam was a good investment. Inflation dropped from 487 per cent in 1986 to 10 per cent in June 1994 and the growth rate averaged between 5 and 9 per cent from 1990 to 1995 (Balfour, 206). Vietnam, however, without investor-friendly structures in place, was unable to absorb the overly anxious capital. The issue then, it seems, became one of control. Philippe Colin, Executive Director of Indochina Asset Management which manages the US$65 Million Beta Vietnam Fund 'officially maintains that he is involved only passively in his investment in a water amusement park in Ho Chi Minh city', *Institutional Investor* reports. However, Colin also admits that 'the fund has been involved in every level of planning, right down to what kind of ice cream they plan to serve', he says with obvious satisfaction' (Balfour, 205). Perhaps it is telling that the first director of another prominent fund, the Finansa Thai Vietnam Frontier Fund based in Bangkok, was former Central Intelligence Agency chief, William Colby, who fought covert missions during the Vietnam war (Balfour, 205). Dominic Scriven, managing director of Dragon Capital in Ho Chi Minh City, comments ' ... you need all hands on the pumps to create deals – in starting them up, in developing them, in financing them, in structuring them and in getting permission for them' (Balfour, 206). In addition to controlling the projects directly, *Institutional Investor* listed the remaining changes that Vietnam needed to implement in order to receive the capital being held by the investment community. By stating 'Vietnam is trying to accomplish in the space of a few years what most economies took generations to do,' *Institutional Investor* implies that the process has still been too slow for investors. Commenting that 'only four state companies have been privatized' and 'shares of joint stock companies are off-limits to foreign-registered funds,' the publication served as a useful tool for institutional investors to signal government officials in Vietnam (Balfour, 206).

Investor activism has also increased as local institutional investors have learned they can effect change through proxy voting. In Hungary, investment firms ousted the directors of two of the largest local corporations and attempted to takeover another. Arago, a 'Budapest-based team of corporate raiders', held 15 per cent of Zalakeramia, Hungary's largest ceramics corporation and Central Europe's largest supplier of tiles and bathroomware (*The Economist*, May 1999: 3). Not liking the fall in share prices, Arago persuaded investors to join them in ousting the current director and appointing its own Imre Pataos. Similarly, the Hungarian-based fund management firm, Croesus, and the US-based Templeton, ousted the director of TVK, a Hungary's largest petrochemical company. Croesus, with 35 per cent ownership, joined forces with Templeton and won 97.5 per cent of shareholder votes to appoint a new director from US-based GE Capital, an institutional investment firm (*Central European*, 1999: 8). In another attempt at restructuring, Croesus joined forces with Argus Capital International, a subsidiary of US-based Prudential, to take over Confinec, Central Europe's largest packaging company (*The Economist*, May 1999: 2). The intention in the takeover was to turn the company around presumably in part by selling off less profitable entities and then sell the company in three years or so (2). Some of the largest shareholders, Credit Suisse First Boston and Flemings, were influential in deciding the company's fate.

In Russia, political elites have used foreign institutional shareholder power to maintain their powerful positions in the country's industrial conglomerates. For instance, Anatoly Chubais, Yeltsin's deputy prime minister from 1993 to 1997 and co-architect of Russia's economic reforms, is chairman of Unified Energy Systems (UES), one of Russia's largest corporations. Chubais, in an effort to preserve his position as he runs for President in 2000, increased the power of shareholders within the company's statutes. This maneuver effectively took the power of firing the chairman away from the board of directors and gave it to the shareholders. To remove him from office, 75 per cent of shareholders' votes are needed. Over 30 per cent of UES is held by foreign investors, historically big supporters of Chubais (*Central European*, 1999: 8).

Investor activism, although practiced primarily by individual firms in the above incidences, is being increasingly coordinated through organizations like the Council of Institutional Investors. As described in Chapter 4, one of the Council's primary activities is to act as a vehicle for institutional investors to coordinate their actions to compel underperforming firms to accept shareholder-preferred restructuring strategies. Receiving an annual focus list of firms that the Council deems should perform better; member institutions are able to begin a coordinated program to control corporate actions. Fisher and Sobokin (1995) found that this 'institutional pressure accompanying appearance on a focus list generates real operational results in the corporate community' (6). In other words, the Council's work in facilitating activism was successful in increasing shareholder wealth. The Council has also initiated an international corporate governance networking program which encourages coordinated activism to take place across the globe. A 1996 study reported that US institutional investors will increase their demands on foreign corporations, primarily through proxy voting. This trend has been increasing as debt-financing moves to equity-based financing and privatizations of state-owned enterprises increase.

To be sure, corporate governance can have positive as well as negative effects, often depending on one's viewpoint. For instance, some US shareholder activists have targeted excessive executive compensation and social issues like the environment and health, as areas of concern. Pension fund managers, controlling 30 per cent of US-purchased foreign equity in 1994, for instance, often must abide by investment guidelines set by their corresponding union or corporation (*Corporate Board*, 1996: 29). Some of these rules may prohibit investing in particular countries or industries. However, as social conscientiousness can inhibit profits, most corporate governance strategies do not center on humanitarian concerns.[7] Shareholder activism tends to mirror neoliberal reforms, on a corporate level in the US, or on a corporate or country level in emerging markets. Profit is the main goal with preferences for restructuring strategies that reduce workforces, cut costs, sell marginal enterprises, and fire ineffective managers. As the power large investors have in developing countries increases, previously state owned industries, the lifeblood of some nations, and their corresponding political power, will fall increasingly under this profit-making meritocracy.

Other market influences

Another means by which individual investors can effect policy in emerging market countries is through utilizing alliances and intermediaries like emerging market political and business elites, domestic governments, and international institutions. Institutional investors influence politics in emerging market countries through the alliances they form with domestic political actors and the empowerment that accrues to these domestic actors. Leslie Elliott Armijo suggests that the new inflows of portfolio capital empower certain domestic political actors while weakening others. In her analysis, she sees business elites in particular benefiting from the new private capital flows. In such an event, these alliances are simply serendipitous as institutional investors find themselves aligned with certain elites on policy choices and the symbiosis is accidental. At other times, the relationships are purposely forged to formalize the efforts mutually benefiting one another. For instance, in Indonesia, Merrill Lynch made the brother in-law of Suharto's second oldest daughter, Hashim Djojohadikusumo, their main partner and was later able to win the contract for the initial public offering of two Indonesian telecommunications firms, including PT Telkom. Merrill Lynch received US$17 million in fees for these IPOs (Shari, 1996: 107). Jean-François Seznec's case studies of Kuwait, Bahrain, and Saudi Arabia, suggest that the financial markets in non-democratic countries 'are established not to provide an intermediary institution between supply and demand of captial but as institutions to direct investments to projects and firms that will lead to the maintenance of the political regimes in power.' [8]

An example of the networks that are formed by investors, developing country elites, and international organizations is found in the story about the downfall of Russia's economy. The economic and political landscape in Russia following its demise as the Soviet Union was in a large part shaped by Western economists and consultants. In particular, the role of certain individuals responsible for setting up Russia's reform strategies provides insight into the potential power that large portfolio investors can wield in countries desperate for capital. The following account is an excerpt of the story told by Wedel (1998).

One of the players responsible for the restructuring of the Russian economy was Anatoly Chubais, the former First Deputy Prime Minister appointed by Yeltsin to work with Western advisors to implement a myriad of economic reforms. Following the crisis of Sach's shock therapy reform that began in 1991, Chubais was appointed to save the fate of these reforms. The primary link to the West was the Clinton-designated Harvard Institute for International Development. The Harvard Institute of International Development (HIID) had strong ties within the administration, in particular Lawrence Summers, Deputy Treasury Secretary responsible for much of US policy towards emerging market economies. Andrei Schleifer, a Russian economics professor at Harvard, was appointed as director of HIID's Russia project and Jonathan Hay was made its general director in Moscow. From 1992 to 1996, HIID received US$57.7 million in grants from the US Agency for International Development (USAID) (Wedel, 1998: 12). In addition, they arranged contracts for US$300 million in USAID grants, including US accounting firms and advertising agencies (Wedel, 1998: 13). In addition, in 1992 HIID helped found the Russian Privatization Center (RPC). The RPC, a not-for-profit private organization with Maxim Boycko as Chief Executive Officer, received US$45 million from USAID, US$59 million from the World Bank, US$43 million from the European Bank for Reconstruction and Development, and millions from the European Union (Wedel, 1998: 13). Boycko, in addition, was a colleague of Sheifler and co-authored *Privatizing Russia* with him. In addition to setting up the RPC, HIID helped create other institutions that were critical to investors. The Federal Commission on Securities, created by presidential decree, was funded by two Harvard-created institutes. One of these was the Institute for Law-Based Economy (ILBE), funded by the World Bank and USAID. This institute was set up to help establish the legal infrastructure for Russian markets. Both of these institutes, as well as the Federal Commission on Securities, were created without the approval of the Russian parliament and under the auspices of the HIID. The centerpiece to reform was to open the financial markets to foreign investors by recreating the US blueprint for a securities market.

Wedel argues that these reforms and institutes were instrumental in buttressing the power of the Russian oligarchy. However, in addition to whatever role these organizations played in helping the Russian elites, the activities of these organizations also allowed particular portfolio investors special access to the Russian market. For instance, Hay, HIID's general director, helped his girlfriend set up a mutual fund that was granted the first license by the Federal Commission on Securities. Furthermore, Hay and his girlfriend,

Elizabeth Herbert, Shleifer, and Vasiliev set up a private consulting firm utilizing funds from the ILBE. Furthermore, Shleifer's wife, Nancy Zimmerman, a hedge fund manager that traded heavily in Russian bonds, had privileged access to the activities of these institutes through her husband's positions at HIID and the RPC. Zimmerman's company even set up a Russian corporation with Sergei Shishkin, the chief of ILBE, as its head.

The many activities of HIID and its affiliates demonstrate the incestuous nature of some economic reform programs and the conflicts of interest that can exist in international finance. By setting up a series of private organizations, the HIID advisors and their cronies were able to circumvent the Russian Duma and direct millions of dollars towards the building of a free market infrastructure benefiting domestic and foreign investors. In addition, the people entrusted with the building of this free market infrastructure seem to have violated some of the most basic laws governing a fair market. Utilizing their special status as architects of the new Russian financial markets, these individuals manipulated funds and regulations to benefit particular fund managers for their own gain. This example of the strong ties between Russia's economic program and Western experts on financial matters also represents the type of incursions the investment community is able to make in the politics of economic reform.

Another important intermediary to effect policy changes in emerging market countries is the government of the country in which the institutional investor is domiciled. Large investors frequently lobby, as individual firms or in concert with others, for policy choices at home.[9] While concerted investor efforts to influence governmental policy are described in the previous chapter, it is worth noting the increased efforts of the International Institute of Finance to influence the US position on the components of the international financial architecture. Throughout the deliberations of IMF, World Bank, and G-7 on how to prevent another Asian Crisis, the IIF has been particularly vocal about focusing efforts on reforming existing system, keeping private sector involvement voluntary, and increasing data availability for investors. However, individual institutional investors also can work alone to influence policy. The incident with Riordan Roett, mentioned previously, demonstrates such a phenomenon in which a single firm sought to influence

US government policy towards one of their major investment locations. Representing Chase Manhattan, Roett lobbied major clients and Congress to adopt certain foreign policies prescriptions for Mexico following the peso devaluation. On a more international level, the aforementioned emerging market fund manager, Mark Mobius, urged the world's richest countries to 'severely punish' Malaysian Prime Minister Mohammed Mahathir for enactment of capital controls following the Asian Crisis in 1998 (Mellow, 1998). In the wake of Mahathir actions, Mobius called for a unity of action as he warned, 'If the structure of law and order in the global financial community breaks apart, all bets are off. We have a very, very dangerous situation developing globally' (Mellow, 1998). Mobius pulled US$2 billion dollars out of Malaysia since the imposition of these capital controls. By February 1999, *The Economist* announced 'Malaysia's defiant surrender' as the capital control that inhibited short-term portfolio investments, was lifted (*The Economist*, 1999: 79). Morgan Stanley dropped Malaysia from its influential Morgan Stanley Capital International index following the imposition of these controls but announced in August of 1999 to reinstate Malaysia on 29 February 2000. However, Mobius allegedly led an effort to persuade fund managers to persuade Morgan Stanley to keep Malaysia out of this index. Inclusion in the MSCI index, a benchmark for many emerging market funds, would inevitably bring in new investments as fund managers would not want to risk excluding Malaysia from their own portfolios. In October 1999, Morgan Stanley postponed the reinclusion until 31 May, stating they wanted to avoid potential problems with the leap year. However, the *New York Times* reports Mobius as stating 'Thank God they listened to our advice' (Arnold, 1999: C2). Efforts such as these indicate the increasing tendency and ability of fund managers and large investors to initiate, organize, and impact the policy choices of sovereign leaders. In this incident, investors boycotted a country because of policies intended to protect Malaysia from the 'hot money' that had recently helped to impair their economy. Mahathir's authoritarian style of governance remained a non-issue.

One of the centerpieces of the new international financial architecture is strengthening the legal and regulatory environment for investors. The Corporate Governance initiative, proposed jointly by the World Bank and OECD, seeks to improve shareholder rights within emerging market countries. Although perhaps offering the benefit of improving business oversight and possibly reducing corrupt practices, this initiative would also augment the power of large investors in emerging market politics.

Conclusions

The financial markets in developed countries like the US provide an important framework for understanding the characteristics evolving in the emerging market countries. Central to the similarities between these two capital markets is the growing power of large investors to amplify their preferences and even at times control the outcomes of corporate and governmental policies. The strategies used to realize particular outcomes can range from market manipulations, like front-running, to direct attempts to intervene in the making of economic policies. Practices like front-running, although very difficult to detect even in the much more heavily monitored and regulated US markets, have fertile ground in the much less regulated and less efficient emerging stock markets. In addition, a look at the growing phenomenon of corporate governance in the US offers insight into the growing practice of investor activism taking place in developing countries. Stories like the making of Russia's economic policies illustrate the complex network of domestic elites, international institutions, and government officials at work to support the interests of private financiers.

6
Democratization and the Institutional Investor

As previous parts of this book suggest, institutional investors demand guarantees from sovereign governments. Institutional investors are not looking for a variety of economic or political choice, but rather the speed at which formulaic reforms take place without causing risk to future returns. If a country is committed to maintaining or attracting investments as a national priority, as the primary emerging market countries have been, then speed of reform and the maintenance of stability are crucial. Given the austerity of most reforms and their propensity to cause discontent among the population, are not these two goals at odds with each other? Does then political repression become a necessary means to serve both goals of economic reform and stability? In particular, does the speed and austerity demanded by large investors of the reform process encourage political repression and authoritarianism?

Previous chapters have addressed institutional investor preferences and how these are expressed, encouraging emerging market countries to accept particular policy choices. This chapter looks at how successful some of these processes may have been in influencing political policy choices affecting levels of freedom in the 1980s and 1990s in emerging market countries. In particular, we shall explore the possibility that there is some relationship between the apparent institutional investor preference for stability over democracy and the levels of political rights and civil liberties in emerging market countries. This chapter is divided into three sections:

1. In this section, we first look at some of the work that has been done on economic reforms and democratization, and how finance

capital has changed the context in which this work is grounded. This section briefly speculates on the limitations of two veins of development theory when put into the new context of portfolio capital. The role of the nation-state and relationship between economic growth and democracy are addressed. In addition, five ways in which finance capital has impacted the economic reform process are outlined. The second part of this section presents a brief survey of theorists that have begun to reconfigure development theory by addressing the relationship between portfolio flow increases and democratization in developing countries.

2. Next, we test the hypothesis that institutional investors encourage authoritarianism by analysing data on market capitalization and freedom in emerging markets. Quantitative tests are included that measure the relative rates of change for political rights and civil liberties between those countries with stock markets and those without.

3. Complementing the quantitative analysis, this third section discusses some specific responses of emerging market countries to institutional investors. In particular, it looks at the democratic progress in developing countries under various conditions and comments briefly on cases in which investors may have directly or indirectly impacted particular political rights and civil liberties.

The nation-state and economic reforms in the context of portfolio capital

The theoretical literature available on the political effects of foreign capital penetrations into developing countries is rich. However, much of this development literature, either from the dependency or modernization schools of thought, does not take into account the late twentieth-century shift from public to private financial flows and the impact of institutional investors on emerging markets. In discussing the impact portfolio capital can have on democratization, two of the more important veins of development theory are addressed, the role the state plays in development, and the relationship between economic growth and democratization.

The dependency school of thought and scholars influenced by it, hold that the entrance of foreign capital into developing countries has fostered a climate of dependency in which recipient countries are strongly influenced by the investing countries. Although the relative simplicity of the initial dependency theorists has been sophisticated by arguments that consider the role of domestic actors, the pervading logic is that within developing countries, the nation-state is profoundly influenced by the influx of external financing. In essence, the nation-state is superceded by the powers within the international political economy. Thus, the nation-state becomes less important as the reliance on foreign capital grows.

From a business-minded perspective, many economists support a similar view that the nation-state has diminishing powers. Their view is based on the expansion of a borderless international financial network. For instance, Kenichi Ohmae presents an argument that the nation-state is 'crumbling' because they do not have 'the will, the incentive, the credibility, the tools, or the political base to play an effective role in the borderless economy of today' (1995: 120). He believes the nation-state an 'artifact of the eighteenth and nineteenth centuries' (119).

There has been at least one significant scholarly departure from the idea of the receding state. Peter Evans presents a counterargument to the aforementioned position that the penetration of foreign capital into developing countries will lead to a diminished role of the state in economic activities.[1] He argues that on the contrary, infusions of foreign capital promote the expansion of the state's economic interventions (Evans, 1987: 321). Using three modes in which foreign capital enters the state; through extractive industries, as manufacturing transnational corporations (TNCs), and as loans; Evans demonstrates how each has enabled state enterprise to increase its intervening activities, albeit in different ways in each case.

Evans provides an interesting case for the interrelationship between foreign capital and states' historical propensity to nationalize TNC enterprises, protect local bourgeoisie industries resulting from TNC presence, and play a mediating role between foreign loans and local industrialists seeking loans, as in the case of Korea.[2] Among his conclusions, however, Evans suggests that the state is able to expand its economic role simply because it is able to legitimize its interventions against transnational capital. Using nationalism as a measure of legitimacy, Evans argues the state justifies its growth through the regulation of foreign capital penetrations (Evans, 345).

Although this author agrees with Evans that the state has expanded its powers in many ways, it has been for different reasons than Evans' theories would suggest. If his conclusion that the state can legitimize growth by intervention against foreign capital were true at the time of Evans' writing, it is not the case at the turn of the millennium. First, the implication that the state's expansion has been primarily directed at the regulation of foreign capital has proven to be false. Indeed, developing countries are now in a contest for who can become more attractive to international investors. Opting out of this game can have serious repercussions for developing economies, as many have become dependent on these capital flows. Even in the face of economic turmoil wrought by foreign portfolio investors, emerging markets may enact limited capital controls but retain the ultimate goal of attracting these same investors. Second, it does not follow that the state has expanded simply because it could through de-legitimizing of foreign investments and loans. Even if there was a time when leaders could bank on the political popularity of attacking foreign interventions, this did not necessarily mean regulations would hinder foreign capital more than it would labor or local businesses. In addition, even if tariffs or taxes were directed specifically at foreign capital investments, this increasingly infrequent policy direction is likely to see its end in the next century as competition for funds deepens.

Investments in the late 1990s and into the new millennium are qualitatively different than the capital Evans is speaking of – IMF loans and large TNC industries domiciled in country. Instead, the bulk of foreign capital flowing into developing countries is fickle, rapidly mobile, and highly seductive in its sheer volume. This has created a climate of competition in which developing countries have little room to experiment with or implement needed social reforms. They must present their countries as commodities with all the prerequisites required by the international investment community. Even the suggestion of an expensive welfare expansion program could send millions of dollars elsewhere overnight. Ohmae's borderless world, in which the nation-state's powers are diminished, underestimates the role of the state in packaging and selling countries to institutional investors. Moreover, although governmental budget slashing is an attractive reform to would-be investors, the power growth of nations' finance ministers and central bankers should not be overlooked. Implementing unpopular economic reforms *in order to preserve foreign capital inflows* may indeed require more of a state apparatus. As long as a country's stability and macro-economic statistics matter to large investors, the role of the state is potentially augmented.

The on-set of portfolio capital flows affects another area of political thought, those theories addressing the relationship between economic growth and democratization. Earlier work on the relationship between economic and political processes focused on the need for countries to attain a certain level of economic development in order to sustain democratic institutions (Lipset, 1959; Dahl, 1971). Cross-national studies that show significant correlation between economic development levels and political democracy (Bollen and Jackman, 1985; Burkhart and Lewis-Beck, 1994) support this premise of modernization theory. A related question has been whether economic growth helps or hurts democratic transitions, and more recently consolidations (Arat, 1991; Mainwaring, 1993; Pereira *et al.*, 1993; Gasiorowski, 1994; Haggard and Webb, 1994; Bhalla, 1995). Related to the broad-based question about the correlation between economic growth and democratization across all countries, the questions posed by development theorists are again relevant. Put a little differently but in a similar manner, they ask, what is the relationship between the international political economy dominated by the developed nations and the patterns of economic and political development of developing countries? In both of these schools of knowledge, various theories have linked authoritarianism with the role of foreign capital. For instance, Evans sees the alliance between state, local, and foreign capital as instrumental in the political repression of the urban poor and working classes. Guillermo O'Donnell, and later David Collier, challenged the modernization theorists linkages between economic development and democratization. They drew from the experience of Latin American states in the 1960s and 1970s that experienced serious reversals towards authoritarianism, despite rapid industrialization and economic growth. One of their main arguments cited the relationship between import substitution strategies and authoritarianism.[3]

As noted by Stephan Haggard, central to these and other challenges to modernization literature was evidence of the subordination of labor and the left (Haggard, 1990: 257). States, purportedly, will be able to accrue foreign capital more easily because 'multinationals, banks and such multilateral institutions as the IMF and the World Bank are more likely to invest where labor and the left are controlled' (Haggard, 1990: 258). Haggard argues against the assumption that foreign capital was attracted by a controlled working class, citing that 'manufacturing multinationals were not attracted to Latin America by low wages; their main interest was the domestic market' (Haggard, 1990: 258). The focus for both Evans and Haggard has been almost exclusively on foreign direct investors, and not portfolio capital.[4] This presents some problems now for several reasons. First, the very definition of a multinational has changed in its connotation since the development theories were first introduced. Most often multinational corporations (MNCs) referred to those companies that established operations in other countries in order to capture the domestic market. While this practice is still prevalent today, another dimension has been added to the concept of the MNC. MNCs, or more frequently referred to now as TNCs, are now not just global in their manufacturing bases, but in their financing, sales, and servicing. With the technological advances in communication, increased competition between advanced industrialized countries, centralization and consolidation of transnational corporations, and the establishment of low-wage export manufacturing zones in developing countries, wages began to matter more. This globalization included the increase of export-oriented industrialization (EOI) and TNCs' manufacturing operations in developing countries, thus contributing to the focus on lower wages. The work of the new international division of labor theorists brought attention to the importance of wage suppression and labor repression to corporate profits and country choice (Frobel *et al.*, 1980; Fernandez-Kelley, 1983; Ahumada, 1995).[5] Second, since the focus of these theorists has been almost exclusively on foreign direct investment, with portfolio investments rarely addressed, the preferences, power, and effects of portfolio investors is absent from these analyses.

Another important linkage between portfolio flows and democratization that is frequently underestimated is the impact finance capital has on the economic reform process, and indirectly on democratization. The work that has been done on the relationship between neoliberal economic reforms and democratization in developing countries has contributed significantly to our understanding of privatization, political suppression of labor, and populist politics.[6] Again, what is often left out of this literature is the impact the privatization of capital, and in particular portfolio financing, has had on these reforms. The imposition of a financial market onto the means by which developing countries acquire needed capital has brought about a striking difference from the previous distribution system which was dominated by multilateral lending and grants, and bank loans. The new element is *competition* between developing countries and this competition has dramatically altered the domestic politics in emerging markets in five ways. First, it has intensified, or deepened the reform process. Secondly, it has accelerated the reform process. Thirdly, it has obfuscated or eliminated alternative means of economic development. It is more difficult for countries to opt out of the current global economy's meritocracy than ever before. In addition, the unity between multilateral institutional ideology and institutional investor preferences has grown.[7] When the system encounters crises, such as the Mexican peso devaluation or the Asia crisis of 1997–98, the multilaterals and institutional investors work in tandem to alter elements within this system while still preserving the dominant neoliberal ideology. Fourthly, it has privileged and empowered un-elected technocrats, in particular finance ministers and central bankers, within the domestic politics of developing countries.[8] Fifthly, it has devalued and diluted the meaning of democracy for many countries by highlighting their success or failure to implement economic reforms as the primary criteria by which to judge a country's political merit. This devaluation can also be found in academic literature that focuses attention on the relative benefits of democracy to economic growth while omitting important questions such as what type of economic growth is occurring and at what costs.[9] Other measures that inform us about the quality of life improvements that may result from increased economic growth include relative distributions of wealth, rates of political repression, labor repression, press controls, and pollution rates.[10]

Work that has been done that specifically addresses how the changes in capital inflow composition affect democratization processes in developing countries can be categorized broadly into two perspectives. First are the optimists, those that believe finance capital helps democratization. Second are the pessimists, those who believe finance capital inhibits democratization.[11] The optimistic group, represented by the works of Maxfield and Hoffman (1995), Kingstone (1999), Molano (1995) and Stone (1999), makes the case that the increase in finance capital has positive effects for democratization. The pessimistic perspective, more comparative in its approach, looks at some of the negative consequences of this newer form of capital.

The optimistic perspective, most often heard publicly in speeches by politicians and financiers, is also found in both political economy and comparative academic theories. Maxfield and Hoffman, discussed in Chapter 2, utilize a data set of political events and emerging market ADRs to argue that political events have relatively no impact on emerging market ADR prices. As discussed previously, this logic is problematic because it does not separate out overall cuts to emerging market investments from shifts within emerging market investments.[12] Another problem is that Maxfield and Hoffman utilize only ADR data and this is highly correlated with US stocks. Thus, their results are as likely to be influenced by the Dow Jones industrial average as activity in emerging markets. In addition, no variable is included that indicates investor's confidence that political upheavals will be taken care of promptly and efficiently, as is often the case in more authoritarian regimes.

Another optimist, Peter Kingstone, presents the argument that Brazil's political development is better off because foreign portfolio investors impose a new and much needed discipline on policymakers and politicians. He argues that Brazil will have to pay higher costs for the behavior of its Congress because of the shift in financing from MNCs and Multilateral development banks (MDBs) to private capital. He concedes, in agreement with Armijo (1999), that capital flows to actors less concerned with democracy poses a threat to democratic impulses if those capital flows increase *vis-à-vis* others. Citing the work of dependency theorists, Kingstone also suggests that the institutional investor propensity to disrupt the macroeconomy increases because of their ability to exit quickly and their inability to voice concerns. He states:

> institutional investors are probably more skittish and less informed about local politics than other sources of capital, ... [and]

the stock market can inflict real damage on a developing nation's economy in a very short periods of time (Kingstone, 1995: 5).

For Kingstone, this is a good thing. In contrast to the better informed and slower moving international lending institutions, Kingstone believes that this impending threat of quick exit has helped improve Brazil's governing efficiency without detracting from its democratic consolidations. The basic premise of the argument is that the shift in financing to institutional investors increases the threat of macro-economic instability, thus enabling President Cardoso to force Brazil's otherwise overly-fractured Congress to coalesce more easily around his fiscal agenda. Maintaining Cardoso's fiscal agenda is then seen as equivalent to preserving democracy. Kingstone also sees Cardoso simultaneously able to carry out his social democratic program and 'willing to ignore powerful economic actor's preferences' to maintain this (Kingstone, 1995: 9).

One problem with Kingstone's argument is that he admits that the threat of institutional investors is larger and more able to influence Brazilian politics than previous forms of financing from the MNCs and MDBs. If, as Chapter 3 suggests, these investors happen to prefer stability to democracy, this argument is weakened. Furthermore, he admits that empowering the new actors with less of a stake in democracy is dangerous to democracy. His belief is premised on the assumption that Cardoso's fiscal policies will usher in increased economic well being and thus further consolidate democracy. However, he provides no evidence that this actually occurs. This assumption is grounded in the now rather suspect belief that these reform measures, by raising GDP and cutting deficits, will naturally trickle down to help the remaining Brazilians, the majority of which are poor. As scholars have shown, this does not necessarily occur.[13] Also implicit in Kingstone's argument is the value placed upon institutional investor ability to coerce elected officials in the Brazilian Congress to adopt reform measures they would otherwise vote down. This valuation implicitly favors the discipline imposed by institutional investors over the pluralism of Brazil's Congress. While perhaps inadvertently instrumental in enacting reform measures beneficial to the populace, institutional investor discipline does not rely on popular support. Thus, nothing guarantees that this discipline will be exercised for the greater good in the future. In addition, what is absent in Kingstone's analysis, as well as other analyses of the success of neoliberal reforms, are the economic and social disruptions often caused by neoliberal reforms.[14] For instance, the economic crisis in Asia and Russia caused large investors who were highly leveraged in these areas to pull their money out of Brazil. This contributed to fragility of Brazil's currency in 1998 and the subsequent devaluation of the real shortly thereafter. In a pre-emptive move to save the Brazilian economy, the IMF offered a US$41 billion austerity package in November 1998. However, Cardoso needed to reduce social security and keep labor costs down in order to meet the conditions of the loan. In addition, privatizations such as that of Telebras, the Brazilian telephone company, have had consequences for labor that are often ignored. Repressive measures to control protests against the consequences of privatizations and other features of neoliberal reforms, are also downplayed. For instance, on 29 July 1998, protesters against the unemployment and loss of sovereignty that the privatization of Telebras would bring, were confronted by the Brazilian government:

> the auction did not sit well with thousands of Brazilians. Police fired bullets and tear gas at thousands of demonstrators who set up burning barricades to protest the auction. Witnesses said police fired shots at demonstrators in running street battles; several demonstrators lay injured and bleeding. The protesters – including students, union members and people from Brazil's radical landless movement – vigorously opposed the sale ... (CNNfn, 1998).

Ultimately, in a country professing to have a democracy, policy must eventually win popular support. In February 1999, Cardoso's popularity dropped to 21 per cent (Gopinath, 1999: 8). Kingstone is not alone in his valuation of institutional investor 'discipline'. Randall Stone (1999) and Thomas Friedman (1999) also view the financial markets as important in keeping governments in line.

The group of scholars with a more pessimistic assessment of the impact institutional investors may have on democratization is comprised mostly of case studies in which an increase of emerging market country portfolio inflows has adversely affected areas of democracy. Case studies on Indonesia (Winters, 1999), Mexico (Armijo, 1999;

Elizondo, 1999) and India (Armijo, 1999; Echeverri-Gent, 1999) begin to probe into the particular political ramifications brought on by portfolio capital increases. The problem cited most by this group, the threat or eventuality of a balance of payments crisis, is construed as deterrence against government programs or policies that might upset investors. Paradoxically, however, as we now realize, the large quantities of finance capital supplied by institutional investment firms *increases* the likelihood of a balance-of-payments crisis in the first place. Thus, even in these analyses, the role of the institutional investor is again minimized. The following analysis examines the impact institutional investments have on democratization in developing countries.

Aggregate measures of portfolio flows and democratization

Loss of freedoms in emerging market countries, 1986–94

The late twentieth century is frequently cited for the increases of freedom around the world. However, as Table 6.1 suggests, freedom, as measured by political rights and civil liberties, decreased for those developing countries with the highest rates of private capital inflows. The countries listed in Table 6.1, emerging market countries with stock market capitalization over 3 per cent of GDP and with established stock markets since at least 1989, show declines in both political rights and civil liberties. According to these numbers, political rights have declined by approximately 5 per cent and civil liberties have decreased by approximately 15 per cent.

Of the 20 countries listed, two scores of one occurred in 1986 and none in 1994. Countries such as Argentina, Brazil, India, and Turkey lost significant freedoms in civil liberties. The biggest gains were in the most authoritarian countries – Chile, Korea, Taiwan, and the Philippines. Although a more thorough analysis follows to confirm these findings, this provides a quick glance at the recent history of democratization in emerging market countries.

The relationship between market indices, political rights, and civil liberties

Another interesting measure of the relationship between private portfolio flows and democratization is to track the annual market indices of each emerging market country and their record of freedoms. Using

Table 6.1 Political rights and civil liberties in emerging market countries, 1986–95

Country	Political rights, 1986, or year of market inception	Political rights, 1994	Civil Liberties, 1986, or year of market inception	Civil liberties, 1994
Argentina	2	2	1	3
Brazil	2	2	2	4
Chile	6	2	5	2
China	6	7	6	7
Colombia	2	3	3	4
Egypt, Arab Rep.	4	6	4	6
Greece	2	1	2	3
India	2	4	3	4
Indonesia**	5	7	5	6
Jamaica	2	2	3	3
Jordan	5	4	5	4
Kenya	6	6	5	6
Malaysia	3	4	5	5
Mexico	4	4	4	4
Morocco	4	5	5	5
Nigeria	7	7	5	6
Pakistan	4	3	5	5
Philippines	4	3	2	4
South Africa	5	2	4	3
Thailand	3	3	3	5
Turkey	3	5	4	5
Venezuela	1	3	2	3
Zimbabwe	4	5	6	5
Totals	86	90	89	102
Averages	**3.73913**	**3.913**	**3.86957**	**4.43478**

*Countries that had stock markets open after 1990 were excluded, mainly because the time period was too short and many of the markets were quite small. Some countries (and their market inception dates excluded include the following: Czech Republic, 1993; Ecuador, 1992; Slovak Republic, 1994; Peru, 1992; and Sri Lanka, 1992. None of these countries exhibited much change in political rights or civil liberties between their market inception date and 1994.

** Indonesia opened its stock market in 1989 so freedom rankings are from this year.

Source: Freedom House.

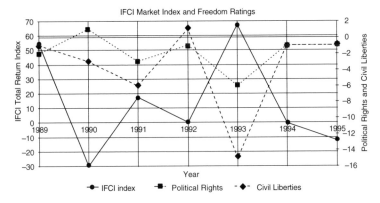

Figure 6.1 Emerging market performance and freedom ratings

Source: IFC and Freedom House.

the Gastil data again to measure political rights and civil liberties from 1989 to 1995, an overall score for emerging market countries' gains and losses was tabulated for each year. Then, using the International Finance Corporation's Global Index, IFCG, the aggregate percent change of total returns was calculated for the same countries during the same time period. Figure 6.1 shows the consistency of the inverted correlation between the two. In almost every case, as political rights and civil liberties decrease, total returns increase. Most notably, 1993 is a year where civil liberties dropped 9 points and political rights dropped 6, and the IFC total return index showed an increase of 67.5 per cent.[15] With only two exceptions, every year shows an inverse relationship between civil liberties and total returns, and, between political rights and total returns.[16]

Regression results for changes in political rights and civil liberties over time

To measure whether or not the presence of a stock market and emerging market status could impact the rate of change of political rights and civil liberties over time, a particular kind of regression analysis was performed for 104 developing countries from 1985 to 1995.[17] The results indicate that the presence of a stock market adversely affects political rights and civil liberties, holding other economic factors constant. For political rights, developing countries without a stock market or with very low market capitalization (less than 5 per cent of GDP) showed signs of increasing their political rights between 1985 and 1995.[18] Developing countries with a stock market that had market capitalization over 5 per cent of GDP, representing the emerging market countries, however, decreased their political rights over the same period.

Constructing counterfactuals for emerging market frreedom rates

Essentially, we want to find out what the rates of freedom would have been for emerging market countries if they were non-emerging; and what the rates of freedom would have been for non-emerging market countries if they were emerging (Przeworski and Limongi, 1996). In order to match cases, or construct counterfactual observations, the observed rates of freedom for emerging market countries were replaced with 'missing' observations indicated by '(.)'. Then, a Heckman selection model is used to control for the effect certain variables (gdp per capita, inflation, foreign reserve assets, and growth rate) may have on whether or not the observation was missing, i.e. whether or not a country was emerging (see Equation 1).[19] In other words, testing for the exogeneity of each x that could effect y (Przeworski and Limongi, 1996: 24). From this model, the potential values for rates of freedom for emerging market countries, had they been *non*-emerging, are predicted. Similarly, the observed rates of freedom for *non*-emerging market are replaced with missing observations and the procedure repeated (Equation 2). Then, the mean of y (freedom rates) is obtained for (1) emerging market countries as observed; (2) emerging market countries had they been non-emerging; and (3) all countries had they been emerging. Similarly, the mean freedom rate (y) for non-emerging market countries was obtained (1) as observed; (2) had they been emerging; and (3) had all countries been non-emerging. The mean for the overall rate of freedom is also calculated. (1) as observed; (2) as if all countries had been emerging; and (3) as if all countries had been non-emerging. The results are shown in Table 6.2.

Table 6.2 indicates that had all countries been non-emerging, the mean freedom rate would have been 0.184, above that of the observed mean (0.147) and above the mean had all countries been emerging (-0.112). In other words, if all countries had stock market capitalization of above 5 per cent of GDP, then their rate of

Table 6.2 Mean predicted values of freedom rates for emerging and non-emerging countries under observed and counterfactual conditions

	As observed	All countries emerging	All countries non-emerging
Overall freedom rate	0.1471215	−0.0116612	0.1838819
Emerging countries	0.0101523	0.0972222	0.3674562
Non-emerging countries	0.1835358	−0.0418717	0.132948

Table 6.3 Mean rates of change for political rights and civil liberties, emerging and non-emerging market countries, 1985–94

Country status	Emerging markets		Non-emerging markets	
Measure	Mean	Std Dev.	Mean	Std Dev.
Political rights	0.0104	0.8416	0.1407	0.7858
Civil liberties	0.0052	0.5448	0.1158621	0.7304

democratization would be on the average approximately 16 times less than if all countries had stock market capitalization under 5 per cent. In addition, emerging market countries had higher mean freedom rates when observed as non-emerging (0.133) than as observed (0.010) or as if all countries were emerging (0.097). Non-emerging market countries showed a negative mean freedom rate when observed as emerging (0−.042), but positive when all countries are non-emerging (−0.368) and positive as observed (0.184).

These results support the hypothesis that the finance capital inflows of the 1980s and 1990s do not have a positive effect on democracy. In fact, these results indicate that emerging market countries are more likely to lose political rights and civil liberties over time, than those countries without the large influxes of this type of capital. This suggests that the mechanisms for finance capital distribution and the subsequent responses of those countries most reliant on this capital could inhibit political liberalization and possibly encourage political repression.

In addition to the general measure of freedom during this period, Table 6.3 is a breakdown of the rates of change for political rights and civil liberties.

As Table 6.3 indicates, both political rights and civil liberties show a much lower rate of increase in emerging market countries than non-emerging market countries. Non-emerging market countries show a rate of increase of political rights 14 times higher than that of emerging market countries. Similarly, civil liberties appear to increase at a rate 23 times greater in non-emerging market countries. The higher rate of increase in non-emerging market civil liberties may have important implications. As stated previously, it is sometimes difficult to ascertain the level of democraticness of those countries trying to attract investors because they may often produce symbolic gestures of democracy while retreating from implementing more substantive measures. For instance, elections, arguably one of the most visible symbols of democracy, may be conceded and publicized while civil liberties are more quietly curtailed.

Although these tests make a case that portfolio capital has not been beneficial to democratization in the established emerging market countries, making a direct correlation between the level of market capitalization and democratization is problematic for a variety of reasons. First, there are numerous factors that can influence the level of market capitalization of any country, many of which are exogenous to domestic politics, as discussed in Chapter 2. Interest rates in the US, currency problems in a neighboring country, and political instability in a region are among those factors that can impact a country's stock market regardless of domestic political or economic factors. Secondly, democratization is difficult to measure even if one can agree on a definition, which also poses a problem. Reducing it to a scaled variable dependent on levels of capitalization is a troublesome task. Thirdly, market capitalization and domestic politics are so interrelated that compressing them into a unidirectional causal relationship poses problems as well. Thus, to supplement this quantitative work, the following section provides some brief sketches of regional and country-level political choices related to portfolio investment flows.

Responses from developing countries

Aggregate data analysis helps to flush out some of the potential trends occurring among the emerging market countries, however, it does not shed much light on individual country's policy choices and interactions with institutional investors. In order to get at some of the more particular processes occurring at the level of the nation-state, a case study approach is warranted. Although this book's primary focus is the practice of institutional investors and their impact on developing countries as an aggregate, this section provides a brief look into the impact the changing global capital markets has had on some policy areas and regions.

As aforementioned, one of the reasons it is difficult to determine whether the increase in private capital has an affect on democracy is that it behooves emerging market countries to produce symbols of democracy while assuring stability to private financiers. These assurances are often at the expense of substantive democratic measures such as income redistribution, freedom of the press, and social programs. A closer look at the actions of several emerging market countries will show that governments, in an effort to please institutional investors, will often implement unpopular reforms, forego popular mandates, and circumvent civic participation.

The transformation in the late 1980s in capital inflows to developing countries has precipitated a number of responses by the sovereign state. Governments once directly responsible for the distribution of foreign capital now seek news ways to facilitate and regulate the commerce of capital. Economic policies, which make the private sector more attractive to international investors, are actively pursued. Privatization, trade liberalization, and currency stabilization have rapidly become the modus operandi of LDC governments trying to cooperate with the norms of international finance. For instance, countries are divulging macro and microeconomic statistics and rewriting their corporate rules to become more investor-friendly. Abiding by the rules of transparency and accountability are a direct response to investor preferences. Privatizations have taken place across the globe at an accelerated rate and this is in part because a company cannot 'go public' if it is owned by the state. In addition, central bank policy in most developing countries is now profoundly influenced by the perceptions of currency traders and large investors.

Another type of response is characterized by political and bureaucratic reformations that take place because of the reaction, real or anticipated, of large investors or currency traders. Firing finance ministers, replacing central bankers, restructuring cabinets to please foreign capital, for instance, is now common.

Creating a particular image and changing the perceptions of the investment community is another emerging market activity. Emerging market countries have begun to put much more time and money into creating an image for themselves in the finance world. Hiring spin-doctors, advertising in the *Wall Street Journal* and other trade publications, and doing public relations tours, are now considered part of good finance policy. Those governments that have been unable, or unwilling, to impose rapid liberalization policies often seek alternative means to attract the growing inflow of international private capital and mitigate investor turn-offs. This can sometimes be effective if carried out properly.[20]

Changes in capital flows have produced another response that is political in nature and stems primarily from the perception of loss of power or revenues as foreign financing bypasses the sovereign. For instance, regimes whose political futures are perceived as threatened, will seek to minimize the capital flows to those sectors competing for power within the state. In addition, a deeper level of political control, such as the repression of rebels in Chiapas and the suspension of political rights and civil liberties, may be perceived as needed to enforce economic reforms and retain power.

Of course, although these trends are presented separately, they exist in different combinations and levels in all countries. Countries that play by most of the rules will also try to lobby and solicit capital by other means. In addition, perceived moves against the investment community, like in the case of Mexico's devaluation of the peso, can be considered moves of autonomy yet are difficult to classify as anti-investment because of their professed long-term objectives. Moreover, even if an emerging market does almost everything right, Mexico demonstrated that 'with more than US$1 trillion looking for a home in the foreign exchange market every day, even a slight deviation from the straight and narrow can invite a savaging' (Glasgall, 1995: 55). In addition, there are no guarantees that abiding by certain rules will insure capital flows given the presence of other external factors.[21]

Crises: Mexico, Malaysia, Peru, Brazil

The ability of institutional investors to influence policy choices is particularly visible during crisis periods. Although frequently trying to court the favor of large investment firms during political and economic crises, leaders are also more apt to voice their discontent with the constraints imposed upon them by portfolio capital. In addition, the pressure investors exert upon countries in crisis to adopt certain measures and the response of those countries to this pressure is more likely to be visible given increased media coverage. The period following the devaluation of the peso in Mexico provides some insight on the interrelationship between finance capital and politics, and the non-democratic results that can be produced by pressure from the institutional investor community. Other devaluations, like Russia's in 1997, Malaysia's in 1997, and Brazil's in 1999, reveal similar windows onto the responses emerging market country leaders have towards investor pressure and preferences. In addition, second-tier emerging market countries like Peru, in another type of crisis, can exhibit similar symptoms of being constrained by their need for approval by investors.

Mexico's recovery plan after the peso crisis in 1995

The case of Mexico, one of the first favorites of the emerging market investors, shows that even if a country follows all the rules and investments roll in, governments are not insulated from crises. In fact, investor demands called for increased austerity and civil control. Being overly popular in the emerging markets is one of the biggest reasons for Mexico's troubles in 1995, as well as Asia's in 1998 and Brazil's in 1999. The major institutional investors (foreign and domestic) and their 'lemming-like bent to overlend in emerging markets' (McKinnon, 1995: A29) have been cited as the reason for Mexico's current-account deficit and subsequent inability to support the peso during this period. Mexico's recovery plan, announced in January 1995 following the dramatic fall of the peso, is an example of how investors influenced the public policies of an emerging country, as well as the economic and social well being of its people.

The core of Zedillo's recovery plan was aimed at calming the fears of international private investors. Zedillo's principle behind his rescue plan was simple – 'a big squeeze on the economy to keep the powerful forces of global money at bay' (Smith and Mackin, 1995: 43). The measures in this recovery plan were aimed at reducing the wages of laborers, cutting back on the government's social spending, and selling Mexican property to foreign investors. A control on wages was proposed which would cut the real income of workers whose compensation was already 10 per cent lower than 1980 levels (Smith and Mackin, 1995: 45). However, with 1 million new workers entering the labor force per annum, the Authentic Labor Front

(FAT), a confederation of independent labor unions in Mexico predicted that 'most workers will have no choice but to go along'.[22] In addition to the cut in real wages, Zedillo's plan included reducing the 1995 budget by US$5 billion and cutting the current account deficit in half. These moves, aimed at restoring investor confidence, triggered a recession that endangered the smaller and weaker Mexican businesses. Social spending was slashed as well (Smith and Mackin, 1995: 43).

Even with the successful implementation of wage restraints and budget reductions, a major rescue package of dollars was needed to stabilize the peso and keep investors coming. Zedillo put out requests to the industrialized countries for a stabilization package and awaited billions of dollars of rescue. However, as one Western banker commented threateningly about the rescue package, 'if Zedillo doesn't get his act together "the markets will blow right by $18 billion as if it were a rounding error"' (Smith, 1994: 44). The investment community wanted more than austerity plans and controls on domestic business and labor, they also demanded collateral. In essence, investors demanded a larger piece of Mexico than the privatization reforms to date had provided.

Privatization became the ticket to Mexico's redemption with international investors. Given the memory of the debt crisis of the 1980s, fund managers demanded collateral. Zedillo offered investors Mexico's ports, railroads, local telephone companies, and satellite telecommunications. Insufficient to appease investors, pressure was put on by the major international banks and fund managers to open up Mexico's petrochemical industry, refining operations, and electricity providers. In particular, Pemex, Mexico's national oil company and some say national pride, was coveted.

Privatization, in this sense, did not so much mean freedom from government inefficiencies, but loss of an industry to foreign investors. Foreign ownership in Mexico, as in many other developing countries, is not subject to the same labor laws that are practiced in their countries of origin. In fact, the move of transnational corporations into the developing world is linked with its ability to pay workers less, pollute more, and avoid those laws aimed at protecting the safety and rights of the community in which it operates. This angle was rarely addressed in those journals or television reports that suggested that Mexico should sacrifice its national industries.

As the Mexican drama unfolded, other emerging market countries relying on foreign investments were affected. Because of the tendency of institutional investors to group most emerging countries in the same general 'risk' category, a perceived failure in one has repercussions for many. And with the rapidity in capital movements, this can mean a crisis of great social consequences for developing countries who are relying more and more on the whims of the institutional investor. More severe economic reforms are likely to be implemented in times of crisis, with the need for authoritarian measures increasing rather than decreasing. The actions of the Zedillo government following the devaluation of the peso represent some of the political ramifications that occurred specifically because of the new means of financing.

After the Mexican devaluation, many countries in Latin America experienced the Tequila effect in which they all suffered investment withdrawals because of the decreased lack of investor confidence associated with the region. However, most Asian countries remained relatively unscathed and in fact, seemed somewhat insulated from such a crisis. Dr Mahathir, Malaysia's Prime Minister, recalled this belief in October of 1997, following the devaluation of the Malaysian ringgit:

> And of course we in Malaysia had laughed at the suggestions that our country would follow the fate of Mexico. How could that happen when our economy was so sound? We had practically no foreign debts. Our growth rate was high, inflation low. Politically we were stable and socially harmonious. We had put in place, tried and tested strategies for a continuous thirty-year growth plan (Mahathir, 1997: 2).

The fate of Malaysia a few years after Mexico, as well as other Asian nations, is now part of global financial history. Malaysia and most other Asian nations suffered a fate worse than Mexico. Dr Mahathir, one of the strongest voices in the developing world against the power of institutional investors, makes a case against the role fund managers played in these devaluations. He states:

> we know now that even as Mexico's economic crash was manipulated and made to crash, the economies of other developing countries, too, can be suddenly manipulated and forced to bow

to the great fund managers who have now come to be the people to decide who should prosper and who shouldn't (Mahathir, 1997: 1).

Other instances exist in which certain economic policies are chosen that would appease large investors, despite significant political opposition. On 13 January 1999, President Cardoso announced that Brazil would allow the real to float within a specified band, thus allowing it to devalue. This announcement came after the IMF granted a US$41.5 billion package to avoid another Asian crisis in Latin America. Investors believed Cardoso's newly formed government was too slow implementing economic reform measures and currency speculators began to drive the value of the real down. This forced Brazilian officials to devalue the real, creating an immediate spiral downward as investors feared future devaluation. The *New York Times* reported:

> Brazilian officials have argued repeatedly in recent days that the devaluation was not their fault, but was forced upon them by currency speculators seeking to exploit delays in the adoption of the reform program (Sanger, 1999: C4).

Fortunately, on 2 February 1999, the Brazilian stock market experienced a considerable upsurge when George Soros announced to the world that he believed the real was oversold. Again, in this case, the fate of the country was determined not by economic policies or projections for growth, but, at least in the short-term, governed by the voice of one powerful investor. And, heads of state and finance ministers are increasingly aware of the importance of attracting foreign capital inflows through large investment firms. One government official from Mexico noted that on his trips to the United States he now meets not only with US government officials and development bank representatives, but also with 'twenty-nine year olds in tennis shoes', referring to the younger bond traders in New York.[23]

As central banks and ministries of finance gain more power within the structures of government, lobbying for the monetary and fiscal policies most attractive to foreign investors has become stronger. Clashes between the neoliberal expectations of international investors and the domestic politics have led to conflict. In September of 1998, for instance, Colombia's civil servants led a strike in which hundreds of thousands protested President Andres Pastrana's austerity program implemented to maintain foreign capital financing of Colombia's debt. Strikes and protests to austerity programs have become the norm in many emerging market countries.

Other types of political crises also provide windows into the relative success institutional investors have had in imposing their policy preferences. Trying to calm the fears of investors after the taking of the Japanese embassy in Peru, Fujimori portrayed the crisis at a press conference as 'an isolated event that is not going to upset the Peruvian economy [and] ... an illusion to those who feel this will sabotage the Government, the state and its efforts to attract investment' (Sims, 1997: 8). Merrill Lynch lowered its growth estimate for Peru's economy from over 5 per cent to 4.5 per cent because of the prediction that the hostage crisis would discourage small and medium investors (Sims, 1997: 8). Fujimori criticized those voicing empathy with Tupac Amaru in stating 'You have to ask them if they have some magical formula to win investment in a disordered and violent country' (Schemo, 1997: 8). This statement reflects Fujimori's belief, which mirrors that of the investment community, that an authoritarian government is vital in attracting investment to Peru.

Democratization in non-emerging markets

Developing countries not so attractive to large investors that have implemented substantive political liberalization provide some interesting insights into the relationship between democratization and finance capital flows. For instance, in Namibia elections were held for the first time in 1989. Other countries virtually unknown to institutional investors, like Benin, Cape Verde, Sao Tome and Principe, and Zambia, had multiparty elections in the late eighties as well. In Asia, the Philippines overthrew Marcos in 1985, before the Philippines became an attractive addition to international portfolios. Mongolians established a multiparty system in 1990 without any substantial finance capital. Nepal held elections in 1991 for the first time in 30 years and Samoa held its first elections. Cambodia seems to be making strides slowly and Bangladesh, still out of favor with investors despite great efforts, changed from military rule to an elected parliamentary system. In addition, Jordan realized a national charter ensuring a multiparty system while Algeria and Yemen made significant strides towards democratic rule. Moreover, one of the most memorable shifts towards democracy was the fall of the Berlin Wall in 1989, after which many Eastern European countries began transitions to democracy and *before* they began to court institutional portfolio investors.

Democracy in three emerging markets: Chile, South Korea, and South Africa

Proponents of the political benefits of open financial markets often cite emerging market countries that have moved from authoritarian to democratic governments as examples of the positive impact of neoliberal reform and private capital (de Vries, 1990; Friedman, 1999). For instance, those countries with large foreign capital inflows that experienced significant moves towards democracy include Chile in 1988, South Korea in 1988, and the particular case of South Africa in the 1980s. The case of Chile provides an example of a country that experienced heavy inflows of foreign capital during an authoritarian regime, followed by record economic growth, and the eventual democratization of the political processes. The end of the Pinochet regime provided evidence supporting the virtuous cycle theory that proposes that economic growth does eventually lead to democracy.[24] By extension, it could be argued that the authoritarian nature of the Pinochet regime was an essential component of Chile's economic success, and thus a vital factor in achieving a stable democracy. South Korea is also often cited as an example of a country that achieved economic success and pleased investors under a more authoritarian form of government and then, in the late 1980s, democratized. Furthermore, as is now realized, the nature of South Korean economic reforms was not grounded in neoliberal ideals. In the Chilean and South Korean cases, the moves towards democracy that followed intense periods of successful economic growth, were in spite of institutional investment concerns and have yet to be tested in an environment of prolonged foreign capital diminishment.[25] In addition, most of the funds flowing into Chile and South Korea prior to democratization were composed of FDI, not institutional portfolio flows. Moreover, the attractiveness of Chile as a portfolio investment has been less than remarkable in the years since democratization. According to the largest US mutual fund specializing in Chile, the Chile Fund, 'Chilean equities [were] one of the worst performing markets in 1996' (*Chile Fund Quarterly Review*, June 1997: 1). Although seemingly unlikely, if the Chilean market experienced a long enough downturn of portfolio flows, would its relatively new democratic institutions remain intact? The case of South Africa also demonstrates the precariousness of democratic reforms within the era of private financing. The success of the African National Congress is often seen as hinged upon its ability to lure foreign investors. One editorial in the *Financial Times* recognizes this by stating:

> The ANC's determination to eradicate the consequences of apartheid will set the political debate for as long as it remains in office. But the new arbiters of that debate; which will dictate the policy compromises, are international investors in general and the currency market in part (*Financial Times*, editorial, 21 May 1996).

As stated, South Africa has responded in various ways to the power of international investors. For instance, in December 1994, South Africa was rated below investment grade by S&P's and most risk analysts warned of the uncertain political climate. However, when Mandela issued the first international bond of the post-apartheid government, *The Economist* reports that 'investors seem not to have worried'. This seems to have been due in a large part to an international public relations tour staged by the finance minister and the Reserve Bank governor.[26] However, by the second quarter of 1998, the investment community's enthusiasm for South Africa had waned considerably. The Johannesburg Stock Exchange showed dramatic declines and the South African currency plummeted as traders and investors shied away from emerging markets. South Africa's problems were compounded by the coming elections and the uncertainty that these brought to the financial markets. The *Financial Times* also faulted South Africa's new system of federalism by calling it 'inept and often corrupt, squandering the money carefully husbanded by the central government as part of its investor-friendly commitment to deficit reduction and free-market orthodoxy' (*Financial Times*, 1998).

Whether it is South Africa's old apartheid government or Pinochet's Chile, however, as discussed in Chapter 3, substantial evidence suggests that authoritarianism in and of itself is not any better at implementing economic reforms or achieving desired economic results. As Karen Remmer and others have indicated, the most relevant factor to successful economic reform, is regime *change* rather than regime *type*. Newly elected or newly formed governments, she argues, enjoy a honeymoon period enabling them to implement otherwise very unpopular reforms (Remmer, 1989: 106). However, even if Remmer was wrong, and authoritarianism *was* more apt at implementing economic reforms and reaching democracy through economic growth, little evidence supports the argument that the current financial markets are kind to newly democratizing nations.

India: delinking human rights from investments

Previously in this book, the popularity of India in 1995 as a top emerging market was noted. Coinciding with Commerce Secretary Ron Brown's upcoming visit, India's attractiveness as an investment option grew. The press coverage of India leading up to Brown's visit represents a persistent trend in the foreign policy of industrialized countries, the delinking of trade and investment policy from human rights policy. With increasing popularity among the business community, India's government was reviewed favorably by *Business Week* as they noted India's 'full-throated democracy' as one of the reasons for its capital magnetism.

Other coverage of Brown's trip brought a more critical perspective to the public. In the same week, a *New York Times* article ran the following subtitle for a report on the state of India's democracy: 'Killings. Torture. Vote fraud. When does it become a police state?'. Within the same article critics of India's democracy are quoted as saying:

> India belongs as much in the camp of nations whose governments abuse their people as it does in the club of authentically democratic nations.

and:

> Democracy in India has become like one of those western movie sets – all façade ... and nothing behind it.[27]

The *New York Times* article questioned the reality of India's democracy in the aftermath of President Clinton's decision not to include human rights issues in trade talks. Both these articles followed Brown's trip to India to encourage more business ventures with US companies. Ravi Nair, executive director of the South Asian Human Rights Documentation Center in New Delhi, expressed dismay that Brown, following instructions, did not make any statements about India's abuse record. Nair reports disappointment because 'international scrutiny is the only thing that keeps the situation in India from getting worse' (Burns, 1995: 6). In order for countries to maintain their image of stability, suppressing human rights reports will most likely become more important. Governments in industrialized, indebted countries like the US, that rely increasingly on banks and institutional investors for political support, are not likely to press the issue of human rights in the future. Foreign investors, eager to guard their investments, are most likely to downplay human rights abuses as well. It is unlikely with the growth of private investment that human rights abuses will gain press coverage, or the industrialized countries will link explicitly, trade and investment with democratic reform.

The linkage between human rights and institutional investments has been addressed by organizations such as *Human Rights Watch*. In particular, the Asian crisis precipitated a number of human rights violations in the region as economies collapsed and more drastic measures were implemented to maintain attractiveness to foreign investors. Labor rights, for instance, never a great strength for the Asian economies to begin with, were curtailed even further following the crisis. Human Rights Watch reports: 'Workers in most Asian countries were denied or severely restricted in their freedom of association and their right to organise and bargain collectively.... Women and migration workers were particularly vulnerable' (European Institute for Asia Studies, 1998). The combination of downplaying human rights issues by both developed and developing countries with the increased propensity for human rights abuses during financial crises does not bode well for the future of human rights.

Former command economies

The relationship between democratization and capital inflows into Eastern Bloc countries and the former Soviet Union, in particular Russia, is a complex and fascinating one. While this analysis cannot sufficiently describe the experience of every eastern bloc nation and

Russia, an overview of capital flows into these regions over the fifty years provides an interesting backdrop for the current relationship between democracy and institutional investors. In addition, the description in the previous chapter of the particular relationships that developed between Russian economic reformers and US institutions gives an idea of some of the internal responses the Russian government has had to the international finance community.

Andrew Sobel presents an interesting analysis of the integration of the command, and later former command, economies into the global capital markets. Looking at two types of borrowing, loans and bonds, Sobel finds that most command economies were relatively successful in accessing foreign capital, primarily loans, during the period of détente. Following the Soviet invasion of Afghanistan, during the later Carter years and early Reagan years, East–West relations deteriorated and commercial loans declined. Immediately following the 1989 political and economic liberalization of the command economies, foreign capital inflows increased. However, Sobel cautions that these initial inflows were not as substantial or as pervasive as previously thought. In fact, he notes that the most successful borrower remained China. In addition, Hungary, the Czech Republic, and the Slovak Republics were the only countries who notably increased their foreign capital inflows after the elimination of communism. Essentially, 'most of the former command economies borrowed less than they had before the reforms' (Sobel, 1997: 24). Sobel is quick to point out that this did not represent a decline in need:

> Ironically, access to global capital markets seems to have diminished for many Eastern European nations and former Soviet Republics since the tremendous transformations of the late 1980s and early 1990s. This is not a reduction in demand for global capital from these countries, but reluctance by international investors to lend their capital to borrowers of these nations (Sobel, 1997: 25).

Sobel speculates that the decline in capital access stems from investor uncertainty about the stability of the economic and political environment. Unfortunately, many of the investors' concerns about economic and political stability were realized when the

Russian economy collapsed in 1998. Ironically, prior to this collapse, many speculators had begun betting on Russia and funds had poured in. This Russian market rise was partially due to increased optimism about political stability, but also because speculators believed the international community would never tolerate the threat of a Russian collapse, making a bailout inevitable and reducing investor risk considerably. The overly optimistic lending and investment into Russia contributed to the conditions that led to the demise of the Russian market in August 1998.[28]

The political impact of institutional investors

This chapter has highlighted some of the ways institutional investor power has necessitated a reconfiguration of development theory, impacted democratization in emerging market countries, and changed the actors and landscape of the international system. Rendering previous theories about the state and economic reform outmoded, finance capital's increasing presence in the world requires new thinking about power in the international system and the political consequences of developing countries' reliance on private financiers. Although much attention has been paid to the borderless nature of financial globalization, theories of the state need to incorporate institutional investors' preferences for economic reform and stability and how this effects the state apparatus. Instead of a diminishing, in many respects the state has had to grow in its power, albeit a power that is perhaps only on loan from large investors. Furthermore, how finance capital changes the political economy of the relationship between core and periphery and the nature of economic reform needs to be explored further. The work that has been done on the impact financial globalization has had on democracy has produced at least one consensus; balance of payments crises, often associated with the new rapidly mobile capital, destabilize both authoritarian and democratic governments. However, in the absence of such crises, the daily political processes resulting from increased investor power remains relatively unexamined.

The finding that emerging market countries were more likely to lose political rights and civil liberties than non-emerging market countries uncovers only the tip of the iceberg. The brief survey of the various incidences that have resulted from the growing power of investors illustrates only a few of the possible ways politics have been affected in this new era. The growing political presence of institutional investors during periods of crisis management showcases their power over the fates of these countries and this visibility reinforces tendencies to abide by their preferences. A wave of countries whose destinies remained relatively unlinked to institutional investors' power experienced great strides towards democracy, while others, like South Korea, Chile, South Africa were able to democratize before their countries joined the charmed circle of 'emerging markets'. Emerging market countries as a whole, on the other hand, lost freedoms during the 1980s and 1990s. Countries whose financial ties with the West grew as their emerging markets investments increased, such as India and China, found the battle to expose human rights violations increasingly uphill. After the fall of the Berlin Wall, many of the former command economies began to implement democracy and were surprised to find their inflows of private capital decrease. As they continue to struggle with demands of global capital, their nascent political institutions remain under threat.[29] These glimpses into the erosions of freedom, and policies aimed at helping the poor, extending rights, and redistributing wealth, indicate more is to be discovered about how institutional investors transform the everyday lives of people in developing countries.

Conclusions

The shift away from official development assistance and traditional bank lending to private portfolio capital has wrought many changes in the developing world. In particular, the experiences of those countries most able and willing to court the new forms of private, portfolio capital have been most altered. This shift in the composition of capital flows to private institutional investors has ushered in a new regime of power that is organized by the norms and goals of a few large emerging market investors. I have found that these institutional investors are relatively few, show signs of coordination and, thus, have the capacity, singly and as a unit, to impact the capital flows to developing countries. This power, a distortion to a fair and efficient market system, carries with it the ability to create a meritocracy that rewards and punishes developing countries according to their ability to implement and maintain economic reforms beneficial to foreign investors.

This meritocracy, premised on emerging market fund managers' system of preferences, often values stability at the expense of political democracy. This new dynamic within the international system has set up a framework for development that fewer and fewer countries can afford to ignore. Most emerging market countries try to implement the formulaic reforms demanded by the community of international financiers. The prerequisites for institutional investments, however, consist of not only one-size-fits-all economic reforms, but also the maintenance of political stability. Financial markets dislike uncertainty most and increased political liberalization often appears less certain than the politics of an authoritarian regime. Moreover, these investors will value most a country's ability to implement and maintain neoliberal economic reforms, even in the face of significant popular opposition. Top emerging market fund managers show strong preferences for stability, often at the expense of political democracy. Democracy, as Mark Mobius suggests, is not a necessary condition for investment. And, as Barton Biggs advises, 'it's very helpful to have a dictatorship...' because they '...make the tough decisions and demand the sacrifices...' (Armour and McGowan, 1996: 6). Given institutional investors' preference for stability and the relative devaluation of political democracy, it is not surprising that many of the emerging market countries have lost civil liberties and political rights over the last couple of decades. As mentioned previously, if a country is committed to maintaining or attracting investments as a national priority, as most developing countries are, then speed of reform and the maintenance of stability are crucial. Given the austerity of most reforms and their frequently unpopular nature, implementing reforms and maintaining stability are often at odds with each other and may even prompt repressive measures as in the Nigerian case.

This book has also illustrated how the consensus of the investment community, around reform strategy and political stability, is maintained and emanated systemically through the cohesiveness of this group. The five levels of systemic determinants of investor and emerging market behavior presented; ideological, intra-firm, inter-firm, market, and multinational; reinforce the norms and power of institutional investors.

Individual institutional investors also maintain this criteria through the increasing use of investor activism. Already a prominent feature in the US, emerging markets are increasingly experiencing not only corporate governance, but country governance as well.

The homogenization of reforms, and its constant reinforcement through the myriad of investor networks, perpetuates the oversimplification of reforms and obfuscates the uniqueness of a country's political and economic landscape, and the local needs of communities. Compressing individual countries into aggregate macroeconomic data in order to judge their investment potential *vis-à-vis* others, washes out vital information and eliminates the human element from the investor's view. If a country's stock market is up, the country is looked upon as doing well. Its internal struggles, increasing poverty, or decreasing civil liberties fade into the background or disappear entirely from institutional investors' purview. Government leaders are constrained by the preferences of large investors, often the 'twenty-nine year olds in tennis shoes', that decide the fates of millions. Favoring stability over democracy, austerity over social spending, labor controls over labor rights, status quo over redistributive policies, quiet repression over public demonstration, and millions suffering over losing millions; these investors remain only accountable to their quarterly reports. As one currency trader put it:

> The question of whether that awareness of the consequence for the Indonesian people ... causes you to refrain from an action, is a different thing. Many times, ... the rules of the system exist and if you don't play or if George Soros doesn't play, it doesn't mean the game won't take place. It just means you won't make the money, because somebody else will. You understood it earlier and you could have had the opportunity, but you withdraw from that opportunity, therefore, other people go forward and make the money, and the same suffering takes place. ... Sometimes people feel both like a citizen and like an actor in a game and they're almost compelled to continue to play in the game role, even when it hurts their soul, because they can see the consequences of what this systemic action is producing (Johnson, 1999: 12).

The choice of playing the game, however, poses serious consequences for those countries whose economies and political futures are relying on the profit-maximizing mentality of these investors.

This book has introduced the idea that the change in capital flow composition from official development assistance to portfolio flows has ushered in a new regime structured by the preferences of the financial elite. Although this book has pointed to some of the potential dangers of institutional investor capitalism shaping the politics within developing countries, more work is needed. For example, it would be helpful to have more research on specific incidences in which investor preferences explicitly effected policy changes in the emerging market countries. Furthermore, more work is needed to flush out other aspects of the relationship between portfolio flows and democracy such as the effects of increased private capital inflows on social spending, income redistribution and labor organization. In addition to research on the potential problems of institutional investor power, more work is needed to assess how this power may influence the outcome of various remedies proposed for the maladies of global capitalism. For instance, scholars and institutional investors have proposed increasing the gross domestic savings (GDS) of the developing countries to diminish the power of foreign investors (Feldstein, 1995).[30] In what ways may the spread of investor capitalism change this solution? Also, more analysis of the feasibility of voluntary compliance of investors to an international standard of conduct in investing and trading practices, and the political ramifications of this, is needed.

The argument has been made, by Thomas Friedman and others, that the opening up of capital markets and the behavior of large portfolio investors, unintentionally, had a political liberalizing effect by hastening the downfall of dictators like Suharto (Friedman, 1999). Friedman makes a mistake, however, in his assumptions about the workings of global finance. He believes that the market, open to anyone with a computer, is no longer dominated by a few large investors. In fact, Friedman feels even he has had power over the political destinies of emerging market leaders. Confessing to the Prime Minister of Thailand, Friedman boasts:

'I helped oust your predecessor – and I didn't even know his name. You see, I was sitting home … watching the Thai baht sink (and watching your predecessor completely mismanage your economy). So I called my broker and told him to get me out of East Asian emerging markets. I could have sold you out myself, via the Internet, but I decided to get my broker's advice instead. It's one dollar, one vote, Mr. Prime Minister. How does it feel to have Tom Friedman as a constituent? (Friedman, 1999: 141).

Although Friedman recognizes the power of investment capital in determining politics, he glosses over the role of global capital in sinking the Thai baht. The underlying assumption here is that a currency will sink and investors will leave when leaders do not implement the correct reforms. The market will provide the discipline needed to keep leaders in line, and the market is no longer 'dominated by a 'few dozen banks', but is made up of people such as himself, someone with extra cash and a computer. The reality is, as this book has shown, that the equity and currency markets are still driven by a relative handful of large investors. Moreover, these investors, attracted to those countries that rapidly implement and maintain intense economic reforms while simultaneously controlling political opposition to these measures, often find political democracy not only unnecessary, but also contrary to their interests.

Appendix I Key to Fund and Country Abbreviations

Fund abbreviations

abtr	Abtrust	gt	GT
bari	Barings	klei	Kleinman
bea	BEA	mgm	Montgomery
buch	Buchanan	mgmi	Montgomery Institutional
cl	Crédit Lyonnais	msem	Morgan Stanley
flem	Flemings	murr	Murray
for	Foreign & Colonial	tcw	TCW
gen	Genesis	trow	T.Rowe Price
gov	Govett	temp	Templeton

Country abbreviations

arge	Argentina	mexi	Mexico
braz	Brazil	nige	Nigeria
chil	Chile	peru	Peru
chin	China	phil	Philippines
colo	Colombia	pola	Poland
czec	Czech Republic	port	Portugal
gree	Greece	russ	Russia
hong	Hong Kong	safr	South Africa
hung	Hungary	sing	Singapore
indi	India	taiw	Taiwan
indo	Indonesia	thai	Thailand
isra	Israel	turk	Turkey
kore	Korea	vene	Venezuela
mala	Malaysia	zimb	Zimbabwe

Appendix II Explanation of Statistical Analysis of Emerging Market's Freedom

Regression results for changes in political rights and civil liberties over time

This analysis uses data on 104 developing countries over a ten-year period, from 1985 to 1995. The two dependent variables are changes in political rights (prrate) and changes in civil liberties (clrate).[1] These variables consist of a scaled variable ranking levels of political rights and civil liberties every year, for each country; the scale ranging from 1, the most number of freedoms, to 7, the least number of freedoms.[2] This scaled variable is then converted into rate of change variables by subtracting the next year's score from the previous year's. This second form is the rate of change of political rights (prrate) and civil liberties (clrate) and is recorded so that a change from 2 to 5 would be 3. Thus, decreases in freedom would be negative and increases would be positive. Then, in order to control for a high correlation between political rights and civil liberties, I combined civil liberties and political rights annual changes and called these rates of freedom (fr). These represent the combined rate of change for civil liberties and political rights for emerging market countries (emfr) and non-emerging market countries (nefr).

Independent variables are growth rate (gr), foreign reserve assets (fra), gross domestic product per capita (gdpcap), inflation (inf), emerging market status (ems – a dummy variable with $0 = $ non-emerging and $1 = $ emerging), year, market cap (mcap), and market cap as a percentage of gdp (mcgdp). In addition, since the *rate of change* in cl or pr is utilized, the annual ratings, cl and pr, are used as independent variables to set a baseline for comparison.[3]

What I want to know is if market capitalization as a percentage of gdp (mcgdp) matters in the rate of change in political rights and civil liberties. However, running a simple OLS on emerging market countries would produce results with a selection bias. In other words, if I want to find out if high rates of market capitalization have an effect on freedom, it is necessary to include those countries without high rates of market capitalization in order not to skew the results. The non-randomness of the sample would bias the results. A way to control for this is to construct counterfactuals and run a regression with a Heckman selection model. First, I generate an equation for non-emerging market countries (where ems = 0, or market cap < 0.05); obtain the coefficients on my independent variables, and use this equation to predict the values for freedom rates (y) for all, non-emerging, and emerging countries. This gives the freedom rates for emerging market countries under the conditions of non-emerging ones, or counterfactual observations.

Secondly, utilizing this same method, an equation for emerging market countries (where ems = 1, or market cap > 0.05) is generated and used to predict the values for freedom rates (y) for all, non-emerging, and emerging countries. In other words, to find out what freedom rates would look like if all countries were emerging. Thirdly, statistics are generated for the whole data set as observed. The problems inherent in using two different data sets are thus resolved by comparing 'matched' cases.[4] In addition, using a Heckman selection model, which runs a probit for each equation of interest to determine why some observations are 'missing', controls for the possibility of a spurious correlation like that which could occur between economic growth, levels of democracy, and emerging market status.

After these three steps, the means of the predicted values, generated from equation (1), equation (2), and as observed, are compared to see if freedom rates differ in emerging and non-emerging countries. The differences indicating if the level of market capitalization as a percent of GDP matters to rates of democratization.

The first equation of interest is:

$$nefr = year + prcl + gr + gdpcap + mcgdp + fra + inf + constant$$

This represents my first equation of interest, with non-emerging markets' freedom rates (nefr) as the dependent variable and year, political rights civil liberties (prcl), annual growth rate (gr), gdp per capita (gdpcap), market capitalization as a percent of gdp (mcgdp), foreign reserve assets (fra) and inflation (inf) as my independent variables.

The second part to the first equation is a probit estimate that tells me why certain observations are missing for my dependent variable (nefr, non-emerging market freedom rate), by looking at specific independent variables that might be influencing the status of whether or not a country is emerging, or in this case, has a market capitalization over 5 per cent.[5] The independent variables used in this probit are as follows:

$$Probit\ (1):\ (nefr) = year + inf + fra + gdpcap + gr$$

This equation helped to determine how much time (year), inflation (inf), foreign reserve assets (fra), gdp per capita (gdpcap), and growth rate (gr) help determine emerging market status.

After obtaining the bias-adjusted coefficients for the first equation of interest, I generate the predicted values of rates of freedom for all, non-emerging market, emerging market countries. This represents what freedom rates would look like if all countries were non-emerging, thus constructing counterfactual observations for emerging markets as if they were not emerging, i.e. had market capitalization under 5 per cent of GDP, etc.

Next, the above equation (1) is repeated with emerging market countries' coefficients replacing non-emerging ones, creating equation of interest (2), and probit equation (2)

Equation (2): $Emfr = year + prcl + gr + gdpcap + mcgdp + fra + inf + constant$

Probit (2): $(emfr) = year + inf + fra + gdpcap + gr$

If the rates of freedom for equation (2), a condition of all countries emerging, are predicted to be significantly less than those predicted by equation (1), a condition in which all countries are non-emerging, then this would indicate that higher rates of market capitalization are not only not helpful but perhaps harmful to political rights and civil liberties.

Results

The results comparing predicted values for rates of freedom between emerging and non-emerging market countries using the construction of counterfactuals and the Heckman selection model, show the mean of the predicted values for freedom rates constructed as if all countries are non-emerging is 0.1839 which is significantly higher than -0.0117, the mean of predicted freedom rates if all countries were emerging. This indicates emerging markets could, on average, be more apt to lose freedoms over time and those countries with relatively little or no stock market are more apt to gain freedoms over time. Included below are the commands and output of Stata data (log), with the results presented in table format. Explanations of each command (in parentheses below commands/equations), a key to abbreviations (in italics), and titles for particular output (bolded) have been inserted for clarity. In addition, following the Heckman output are summary statistics for rates of freedom for each equation as well as summary statistics for political rights and civil liberties rates as observed for emerging and non-emerging countries. Comparisons of the mean values within these summary statistics can be found in Table 6.2 and 6.3 respectively.

Procedures used for constructing counterfactuals using Heckman selection model

Equation (1)

(1) . eq nefr year gr gdpcap fra inf prcl

(Equation of interest (1), with non-emerging market's freedom rate (nefr) as the dependent variable and year, growth rate (gr), gdp per capita (gdpcap), foreign reserve assets (fra), annual inflation (inf), political rights and civil liberties (prcl) as the independent variables.)

(1) . eq probit: year inf fra gdpcap gr mc

(Probit equation (1) to determine why certain observations are missing for dependent variable (nefr). in other words, how much time (year), inflation (inf), foreign reserve assets (fra), gdp per capita (gdpcap), growth rate (gr), and size of market capitalization (mc) help determine emerging market status.

(1) . heckman nefr probit, trace

(Running Heckman Model)

Results for Heckman (1): (probit estimates reported first)

Probit estimates	Number of obs = 663
	chi^2(5) = 160.38
	Prob > chi^2 = 0.0000
Log likelihood = −266.78064	Pseudo R^2 = 0.2311

Probit estimates table for equation (1)

0000BF	Coef.	Std Err	z	P>|z|	(95% Conf. interval)	
year	−0.0939252	0.0220411	−4.261	0.000	−0.1371249	−0.0507255
inf	0.0002519	0.0002852	0.883	0.377	−0.0003071	0.000811
fra	−0.0209059	0.0029754	−7.026	0.000	−0.0267375	−0.0150743
Gdpcap	−0.0003292	0.0000518	−6.354	0.000	−0.0004307	−0.0002277
gr	−0.0618618	0.0114499	−5.403	0.000	−0.0843032	−0.0394205
cons	188.8619	43.88497	4.304	0.000	102.8489	274.8748

Mills' ratio coefficient estimate from regression:

Source	SS	df	MS	
Model	53.7930814	7	7.68472592	Number of obs = 519
Residual	868.033508	511	1.69869571	F(7, 511) = 4.52
				Prob > F = 0.0001
Total	921.82659	518	1.77958801	R^2 = 0.0584

Number of obs = 519
F(7, 511) = 4.52
Prob > F = 0.0001
R^2 = 0.0584
Adj R^2 = 0.0455
Root MSE = 1.3033

Results table for equation of interest (1)

nefr	Coef.	Std Err	t	P>|t|	(95% Conf. interval)	
0000BH	−0.0987978	0.584939	−0.169	0.866	−1.247979	1.050383
year	0.0017394	0.0282447	0.062	0.951	−0.0537506	0.0572294
gr	0.0130849	0.0120679	1.084	0.279	−0.0106239	0.0367936
Gdpcap	−0.0000506	0.0000993	−0.510	0.610	−0.0002456	0.0001444
fra	0.0084405	0.0064873	1.301	0.194	−0.0043046	0.0211856
inf	0.0000217	0.0000764	0.284	0.776	−0.0001284	0.0001718
prcl	−0.0852347	0.0193721	−4.400	0.000	−0.1232935	−0.0471759
cons	−2.649506	56.25356	−0.047	0.962	−113.1662	107.8672

Coefficient of Mills' ratio −0.0987978.
Initial estimate of rho −0.0758036

Equation (2)

(2) . eq emfr year gr gdpcap fra inf prcl

(Equation of interest (2), with non-emerging market's freedom rate (emfr) as the dependent variable and year, growth rate (gr), gdp per capita (gdpcap), foreign reserve assets (fra), annual inflation (inf), political rights and civil liberties (prcl)as the independent variables.)

(2) . eq probit: year inf fra gdpcap gr

(Probit equation (2) to determine why certain observations are missing for dependent variable (emfr). In other words, how much time (year), inflation (inf), foreign reserve assets (fra), gdp per capita (gdpcap), and growth rate (gr) help determine emerging market status.

. heckman emfr probit, trace

(Running Heckman model (2))

Results for Heckman (2): (Probit estimates reported first)
Probit estimates   Number of obs = 663
                                            $chi^2(5) = 160.38$
                                          Prob > chi^2 = 0.0000
Log likelihood = −266.78064   Pseudo R^2 = 0.2311

Probit estimates table for equation (2)

000D0	Coef.	Std Err.	Z	P>|Z|	(95% Conf. interval)	
year	0.0939252	0.0220411	4.261	0.000	0.0507255	0.1371249
inf	−0.0002519	0.0002852	−0.883	0.377	−0.000811	0.0003071
fra	0.0209059	0.0029754	7.026	0.000	0.0150743	0.0267375
Gdpcap	0.0003292	0.0000518	6.354	0.000	0.0002277	0.0004307
gr	0.0618618	0.0114499	5.403	0.000	0.0394205	0.0843032
cons	−188.8619	43.88497	−4.304	0.000	−274.8748	−102.8489

Mills' ratio coefficient estimate from regression

Source	SS	df	MS	
Model	16.0676828	7	2.29538326	Number of obs = 144
				F(7, 511) = 1.87
Residual	166.571206	136	1.22478828	Prob > F = 0.0784
				$R^2 = 0.0880$
Total	182.638889	143	1.27719503	Adj $R^2 = 0.0410$
				Root MSE = 1.1067

Results table for equation of interest (2)

emfr	Coef.	Std Err.	t	P>|t|	[95% Conf. interval]	
0000DS	−2.162003	1.859756	−1.163	0.247	−5.839783	1.515777
year	−0.1475653	0.1302247	−1.133	0.259	−0.4050926	0.1099619
gr	−0.1079244	0.0835135	−1.292	0.198	−0.2730773	0.0572286
Gdpcap	−0.0003525	0.0003891	−0.906	0.367	−0.0011218	0.0004169
fra	−0.0314379	0.0254391	−1.236	0.219	−0.0817452	0.0188694
inf	0.0001918	0.0008	0.240	0.811	−0.0013903	0.0017739
prcl	−0.0883813	0.0317976	−2.779	0.006	−0.1512631	−0.0254996
cons	298.9997	262.9537	1.137	0.258	−221.0072	819.0066

Coefficient of Mills' ratio −2.162003.
Initial estimate of rho −1.953556.

Key: year = year, gdpcap = gross domestic product per capita, gr = growth rate, prcl = political rights + civil liberities, fra = foreign reserve assets, inf = inflation.

Generation of predicted values utilizing above model
. *predict rf1*
(275 missing values generated)
. *predict rfne1 if ems = = 0*
(419 missing values generated)
. *predict rfem1 if ems = = 1*
(794 missing values generated)

Summary statistics for rates of freedom for all (rf1), non-emerging market (rfne1), and emerging market countries (rfem1) generated by equation (1), as if all countries were non-emerging
. summarize rf1 rfne1 rfem1

Variable	Obs	Mean	Std Dev.	Min.	Max.
rf1	663	0.1838819	0.3383136	−0.770375	1.222152
Rfne1	519	0.132948	0.3221088	−0.770375	1.222152
Rfem1	144	0.3674562	0.3326745	−0.6568179	0.9863362

. *predict rf2*
(275 missing values generated)
. *predict rfne2 if ems == 0*
(419 missing values generated)
. *predict rfem2 if ems == 1*
(794 missing values generated)

Summary statistics for rates of freedom for all (rf2), non-emerging market (rfne2), and emerging market countries (rfem2) generated by equation (2), as if all countries were emerging:
. summarize rf2 rfne2 rfem2

Variable	Obs	Mean	Std Dev.	Min.	Max.
rf2	663	−0.0116612	0.3416882	−1.508511	0.9856035
Rfne2	519	−0.0418717	0.3423057	−1.508511	0.9856035
Rfem2	144	0.0972222	0.3174686	−0.4987229	0.9076005

Summary statistics for rates of freedom for all, non-emerging market, and emerging market countries as observed:
. summarize fr nefr emfr

Variable	Obs	Mean	Std Dev.	Min.	Max.
fr	938	0.1471215	1.417868	−9	7
nefr	741	0.1835358	1.485533	−9	7
emfr	197	0.0101523	1.120267	−5	6

Table 6.2 compares the means of the predicted freedom rates for above data sets.

Political rights rates summary statistics for non-emerging market countries

Variable	Obs	Mean	Std Dev.	Min.	Max.
prrate	725	0.1406897	0.7828	−3	4

Political rights rates summary statistics for emerging market countries

Variable	Obs	Mean	Std Dev.	Min.	Max.
prrate	193	0.0103627	0.8415613	−4	4

Civil liberties rates summary statistics for non-emerging market countries

Variable	Obs	Mean	Std Dev.	Min.	Max.
clrate	725	0.1158621	0.7304237	−3	4

Civil liberties rates summary statistics for non-emerging market countries

Variable	Obs	Mean	Std Dev.	Min.	Max.
clrate	193	0.0051813	0.5448376	−1	2

Notes

1 Introduction: Private Investment Flows and Institutional Investors

1. For case studies see Armijo, 1999; Echeverri-Gent, 1999; Elizondo, 1999; Kingstone, 1999; Winters, 1999. Some of these are discussed in Chapter 6.
2. The influence of large investors on the domestic politics, and by extension on IMF policies is not to be underestimated however. Chapter 4 probes this relationship in more depth.
3. For a detailed account of the history of external financing to developing countries, see Eichengreen, 1999; Manzocchi, 1999.
4. From Eng, Lees, and Mauer, 1998.
5. Errunza and Rosenberg (1982) found that dividend yields on developing country stocks samples tended to be higher than developed country stock. This spread shrunk in the 1980s, however. Capital gains and not dividend yields are now thought to be the primary reason for emerging market investment.
6. For more detailed data on the increase in FDI, see IMF (1995). Also, for a more detailed explanation of the increase in FDI, see Graham and Krugman (1993).
7. The publication, *Infrastructure Finance*, circulates to the finance ministers and other government officials of developing countries. It is a spin-off publication from the well-known *Institutional Investor* group. This particular quote is from the article by Perry (1994).
8. This is a quote from Nathan Sandler, senior fixed analyst at Trust Company of the West as quoted in Perry (1994).
9. This representative's privately expressed views were conveyed during a phone conversation on 3 January 2000.
10. Thanks are due to William Clark for his comments on the importance of portfolio investors' enhanced credibility.
11. A more precise definition of a derivative instrument is a 'financial claim with value based on that of the underlying securities' (Eng *et al.*, 1998).
12. The impact of some of Soros' opinions on developing countries is discussed in subsequent chapters.

2 Institutional Investors as Political Actors

1. This global integration, occurring on local, national, and international levels, has had two primary forces behind it. First, the opening up of financial and trade markets has ushered in unprecedented levels of

investments and trade. Secondly, technological advances, particularly in the finance industry, have helped increase the volume as well as the speed of capital transactions. Roberto Chang of the Atlanta Federal Reserve made these two points at a roundtable discussion on integration at the 1999 APSA Annual Meeting in Atlanta, GA.

2. See Chapter 6 for more discussion on Kingstone's argument.

3. Jeffry Frieden (1991) presents a broader argument about capital mobility's impact on policy and political actors.

4. A bid is the price a buyer must pay for a security and an 'ask' price is what the seller is able to charge.

5. Garber argues that in the case of the tulip mania the market did not actually exhibit irrational pricing as a whole. For a survey of rational herding literature, see Devenow and Welch (1995). Mader and Hagin (1983) defend the random walk hypothesis by disputing studies that show predictability in price change volatility by providing rationale for defining volatility as risk by suggesting that more investors will naturally be attracted to less volatile stocks. For a convincing argument why this is not the case, see Fosback (1995).

6. Essentially any type of stock selection analysis is an argument against the random walkers. Econometric and technical analyses look for trends in historical data in order to predict future price directions. Fundamental analysis compares the relative statistics of companies, industries, and countries in order to make forecasts. Included in fundamental analysis would be a company's present earnings and management. For general arguments against random walk theory, see Fosback (1995) and Bernstein (1995).

7. See Howell (1993: 81–2) for a model formulated to take advantage of emerging stock market inefficiencies.

8. Other factors contributing to inefficiency are the relative illiquidity of emerging stock markets, the lack of a well-developed legal system to enforce market rules and the looser accounting standards often present in these markets. See Kumar (1994) for a more detailed discussion of some of these factors.

9. For example, SEC rule 144A has loosened restrictions for developing-country borrowing, thus increasing the portfolio outflows for the US to these countries.

10. Study by MacLeod and Welch cited in Maxfield and Hoffman (1995).

11. Hardouvelis *et al.* (1994: 345–97); also in Maxfield and Hoffman (1995).

12. For more information on studies on push factors, see Hardouvelis *et al.* (1994: 345–97) and Tesar and Werner (1993).

13. This index is also referred to as the IFCC index, or the International Finance Corporation's Composite Index. For a list of countries in this index, see the IFC's *Emerging Stock Market Factbook* (1996).

14. As quoted in Lee (1995). The survey, conducted by Eager Associates, questioned 107 funds about their plans for the next five years. They predicted the largest net increase of pension fund investments to the emerging markets to happen in the next two years.

15. The total in emerging market equities totaled US$160 billion in 1993; US$20 billion were held by US mutual funds (Malas, 1995: 23).
16. This estimate is based on an extrapolation of two statistics. By multiplying the amount invested in emerging market funds in January 1996 (US$1 billion) by 12, and then dividing this by the total amount of equity flows in 1995 (US$22 billion), an estimate of 56 per cent was derived. Unfortunately, statistics were not available for a more accurate 1996 figure.
17. Friedman differentiates somewhat between equity investors and hedge fund managers but groups them both in one category of 'short-term cattle' within the 'Electronic Herd'. He does suggest that there has been a rise in the number of hedge fund managers and this further 'diversification' of the Herd, he argues, is why 'no one is in charge,' and there is 'no one to call' (Friedman, 1999: 93, 95). Friedman, however, seems to contradict himself as he also claims that today's financial markets have also *empowered* individuals in hedge funds, like 'Long-Term Capital Management – a few guys in Greenwich, Connecticut' who were able to '[amass] more financial bets around the world than all the foreign reserves in China.' (Friedman, 1999: 12)
18. This does not include all emerging market funds available to investors. It does, however, represent a significant number of both major and minor funds within the US and Europe.
19. These funds are specifically mandated for investing in emerging market countries. Other funds, such as international and global funds, may invest in emerging market countries but invest in other countries as well – thus making it difficult to break down the amounts flowing specifically to emerging market countries. This also does not include funds that have any regional concentration, such as a Latin American fund, or country funds. However, it should be noted that many of the global and international funds are run by the same institutions and research departments that control the emerging market funds. Information is from Reuters (1996).
20. The institutions controlling the largest portions of the Asian funds are, in order, T. Rowe Price (26 per cent), Merrill Lynch (21.6 per cent) and Fidelity (12.1 per cent). For Latin America, Merrill Lynch (27 per cent), Fidelity (16.5 per cent), and BEA (15.8 per cent). Although country funds were not included in this analysis, a somewhat reduced concentration of assets is expected because of the increasing number of local funds domiciled in developing countries that are being made available for foreign investment.
21. Growth funds are different from 'growth and income' or 'income' funds in that they are primarily equity funds and are considered a higher risk than income funds. Emerging market income funds tend to consist primarily of Brady bonds and other bond issues, and the geographic breakdowns of these funds are different from growth funds.
22. It should be noted that this does not necessarily mean that no allocations were made to these countries since the figures are based on only

the top ten holdings. If all holdings were included these percentages may increase or decrease in magnitude.
23. Wolf (1998) has also done analysis that examines the role of geography in determining financial flows. Here he produces a direct estimate of capital flow sensitivity to distance.
24. This is only an estimate since these figures represent Tokyo's total investments; not just those of their emerging market funds.

3 Institutional Investor Preferences

1. Note that within this chapter the expression of preferences by the investment community is not explicitly linked to policy changes in emerging market countries and that more work is needed in this area.
2. 4 February 1997.
3. For examples of the effectiveness of democracies implementing successful economic reforms, see Williamson, 1994. Surjit Bhalla (1994) supports the argument that political freedoms play a significant role in growth through econometric analysis. Mancur Olson (1994) contends that over the long-run democracy promotes development/growth.
4. In determining what the most important criteria are for choosing countries for a portfolio, I have focused on the most revalent 'top-down' factors in order to get at the relative valuation between political stability and democratic norms. 'Bottom-up' factors, those that evaluate corporate earnings, market share, etc., however, should not be underestimated when choosing individual stocks. In determining what the most important criteria are for choosing countries for a portfolio, I have focused on the most prevalent 'top-down' factors in order to get at the relative valuation between political stability and democratic norms. However, what differentiates emerging market choices from developed country choices comes from top-down analysis.
5. Hartman and Khambata, unlike Jebb, may not have considered the possibility that it may be tough for incumbent governments to maximize both these goals simultaneously.
6. The exact breakdown of those surveyed is: 18 public pension funds, 16 investment managers or banks, 14 university endowment funds, 8 corporate pension plans, 4 church-related pension funds, 4 foundation endowment funds, 1 union pension fund and three others. See *South Africa Investor*, January 1995 for more information on the IRRC survey.
7. Title quote from *Fortune*, vol. 130, 31 October 1994: 54. Original quote was allegedly a favorite phrase of Baron Nathan Rothschild. Mobius reportedly is known to repeat this often (Mellow, 1998).
8. Not all investment advisors were bearish on Brazil. For a much more upbeat assessment of the economic clauses of Brazil's new 1988 constitution, see Rosenn (1991: 1–20) and *passim*.
9. Interview, 25 May 1999.

10. For an excerpt of this letter (dated 13 January 1995), see Cockburn and Silverstein (1995).
11 Reuters reported on 46 emerging market funds but only 34 reported turnover rates.

4   Expression of Preferences: Systems of Investor Knowledge

1. Joseph Petry senior emerging markets analyst, Chemical Bank, personal interview, November 1995.
2. Sirjit Bhalla senior economist, Deutsche Bank, interview, April (1995).
3. See Table 4.2 for more examples of shared backgrounds.
4. A case could be made that the practice of tied aid is directly related to the rate of return. Tied aid has been on the increase. For more official development assistance and donors' economic self-interest, see Orr, 1988; Hancock, 1989; Browne, 1990; Feinberg and Raqtchik, 1991; Griffith, 1991; Pante and Reyes, 1991; and Payer, 1991.
5. For more information on aid conditionality, see United Nations (1994), *The Human Development Report* New York: Oxford University Press: 76.
6. This number of course varies depending on the year. In 1993, for instance, this number was set at US$8626 (IFC, 1995: 2). The World Bank classifies countries into three income categories, low, middle, and high. Emerging markets, according to the World Bank, are those that fall into the low and middle categories.
7. Singapore, South Korea, and Israel are examples of this.
8. For more on Bangladesh's efforts to attract foreign investment, see Chapter 6.
9. These numbers fluctuate for the indexes as some countries are added and some subtracted. The IFC began to include countries more recently such as Russia and Morocco. The IFC, however, is more apt to include smaller or more difficult markets than the other two. Venezuela, for instance, was dropped from the Barings' emerging markets index in 1996 because of the implementation of new capital control regulations.
10. Figures are based on 15 May 1996 weightings as reported in Rademan (1996: 84).
11. Index compilers faced a problem in the case of Hong Kong's turnover to China because China and Hong Kong were listed in separate regions within the indexes. The problem with the government mandate imposed on Malaysian stocks was that Singapore's stock exchange would have been halved immediately within the Europe, Australia, and the Far East (EAFE) index, although this money may have left Malaysia shortly thereafter. The problem was resolved after Banker's Trust manager director for global quantitative investments pointed out to the indexes the wisdom of keeping Malaysia in both the EAFE and EMF indexes simultaneously. See (Rademan, 1996: 86) for more details.

12. While this may seem like a good number of managers given the previous chapters emphasis on fund concentrations, the range of the funds was quite wide. Fund mandates on investment vehicles and geography can be quite different. Even if all funds are Asia-specific, income funds, or funds that primarily invest in bond issues, are grouped with equity-based growth funds and balanced funds. Furthermore, single-country funds like the Korean fund are lumped together with a wide spectrum of regional, foreign, and international funds.

13. It should be noted that this is of course not necessarily a good thing in retrospect given the aftermath of the popping of the Asian speculative bubble.

14. Welch, Bikhchandani and Hirschleifer discuss herding as a general phenomenon in a UCLA working paper. Here the concept of informational cascades is introduced. Also, for an excellent overview of 'rational herding' literature, see Devenow and Welch (1995). Included in the latter is also a bibliography of investor psychology, or 'irrational' herding studies.

15. Interview with Pedro Junquiera, Bank of America Brady bond trader for Brazil, May 1995.

16. Mulford, a leading and oft-quoted expert on the emerging markets, is with CS Boston, one of the largest international investors in the world.

17. This statement is found in the inside cover of the Emerging Markets Trader's Association 1993 *Annual Report*.

18. Quote from an interview with Deputy Director of the EMTA, Kate Campagna, as she was explaining the main functions of the organization. The EMTA was started in 1990 by JP Morgan. It receives the majority of its funding through institutional investors like JPM.

19. This is a quote from the *Emerging Market Traders Association's Annual Report*, 1996. It essentially refers to the efforts of US institutional investors to develop the norms for trading within emerging market countries.

20. This is a quote taken from a CD-ROM entitled 'Associations Unlimited' produced by Gale Research, 1998.

21. For full report, see Council of Institutional Investors' website at http:\\www.cii.com.

22. This is a quote from Dr Josef Ackerman, Co-Chairman of the Steering Committee on Emerging Markets Finance of the Institute of International Finance and a member of the Managing Board of Deutsche Bank AG. See IIF (1999) for full citation and web site.

23. Dennis Anderson, Chief Advisor in the Industry and Energy Department at the World Bank, as quoted in Louise Nameth's 'Development banks search for a new direction' in *Infrastructure Finance* (autumn 1993: 18).

24. See Stone (1999) for a good description of the IMF's activities in Russia.

25. Cumings (1999) gives a detailed account of the benefits Western investment firms received as a result of the IMF's bail-out of Korea in late 1997 and early 1998.

26. The conditions of Mexico's bail-out, described in more detail in Chapter 6, as well as the contingencies of Brazil's, included provisions to implement contentious political reforms such as the privatization of many

state-owned enterprises in Mexico, and social security reform in Brazil. Both of these issues were previously expressed demands of the investment community.

27. Fraga (1996: 54) is skeptical of the role lack of information played in the Mexican crisis: 'and contrary to popular belief, lack of information does not seem to have been a major problem'.

28. For more specifics on the Treasury Group's activities, see Doherty (1998).

29. Quote from Mr Magdi Iskander, Director of World Bank's Private Sector Development Department (Chernoff, 1999).

30. Information on MIGA and its loans was obtained from its web site. For access address, see MIGA (1999).

31. Exceptions to the prohibition of sanctions have been filed by several potential signatories. For instance, The US has petitioned to have an exception made for its sanctions against Cuba.

5 Expression of Preferences: Front-running, Investor Activism, and Other Market Influences

1. Front-running takes place when a trader uses inside information on a pending large share transaction to buy or sell shares before the order is completed and made public. This can cause the price to move up or down unfavorably for the pending order.

2. See Devenhow and Welch (1996).

3. Quote taken from Sesit (1997: p. 3).

4. Found in Useem (1996: 30), footnoted as follows: '*Fortune*, 1993, p. 59; Grant, 1992, p. D2'.

5. See Chapter 6 for more details on these organizations and their leadership.

6. See Chapter 3 for Riordan Roett's recommendation that the Mexican government intervene in elections to ensure a PRI victory.

7. The Calvert Group is a socially responsible fund family. It refuses to invest in corporations or ventures that pollute, involve gambling or tobacco or manufacture arms.

8. This quote is taken from an excerpt of an abstract for a class taught by Seznec at New York University in the fall of 1995 entitled 'The Politics of Finance in the Arabian Gulf'. Seznec also has a book of the same name.

9. See Chapter 4 for an overview of the lobbying activities of the IIF.

6 Democratization and Institutional Investor

1. Evans (1987: 321). In an endnote, Evans suggests other scholars who have argued that foreign capital reduces the overall capacity of third world states. Arguing for the positive effects of TNC penetration Evans suggests George Ball, 'The Promise of the Multinational Corporation' in *Fortune*, 75, no. 6 (1967): 80. For the negative spin, Robert Gilpin (1974).

2. Evans (1987: 345). Evans cites Jeffry Frieden's analysis of Korea's use of transnational loans in Friden (1981).
3. In particular the focus was on the second phase of import substitution in which the state is evermore dependent on foreign capital because of the relative infancy of domestic industries and the lack of revenues from the state.
4. Chapter 1 details some of the important differences between FDI and portfolio investing.
5. Frobel *et al.* (1980) coined the term 'new international division of labor' and saw real wages being reduced by these kinds of global restructurings. Deyo (1990) emphasizes that the EOI model is dependent on low-cost labor. Ahumada (1995) details labor repression and wage reduction in Colombia as a result of these trends.
6. See Haggard (1990) for a good review of some this literature.
7. The phenomenon of the shrinking pool of choices for developing countries is found also in convergence theories, for an example of this see Garrett (1998).
8. For an interesting examination of the power of central bankers and finance ministers see Lissakers (1991) and Solomon (1995).
9. For a good review of this propensity, see Perreira *et al.* (1993).
10. Many of these accompanying factors are addressed in Bello and Rosenfeld (1990).
11. Bernard Cohen provides a relatively neutral perspective in his review of the globalization literature in Cohen (1996).
12. For a more detailed discussion of this argument, see Chapter 2's analysis of market push and pull factors.
13. For a good discussion of the relationship between economic policy and equity, and an explicit recognition of the shortcomings of the IMF's policies, see *Finance & Development* (September 1998). This issue provides summaries of the proceedings of the IMF conference devoted to the topic of economic policy and equity held in June 1998.
14. Consuelo Ahumada (1995) does an excellent job of detailing the detrimental economic and social effects of neoliberal reforms in Colombia.
15. Figures for total returns were obtained from the IFC's. *Emerging Market Factbook* (1966: 55).
16. The two exceptions are 1989–90 when political rights increased and total returns increased, and 1994–95 when political rights remained the same and total returns dropped.
17. For a detailed description of the type of statistical analysis utilized and the reasons for this methodological choice, see Appendix II.
18. Since the Freedom House data measures political rights and civil liberties on a scale of 1–7, free to not-free respectively, regressions using these measures over time would report a negative coefficient on year if things were getting freer.
19. Market capitalization as a percent of GDP was not included because this would, of course, predict the missing observations perfectly.

20. The case of South Africa's public relations tour discussed later in the chapter provides a good example of this. Most finance publications also feature full-page ads or whole advertising sections devoted to promoting the advantages of investing in various countries.
21. See Chapter 2 for a discussion of 'push' factors.
22. Smith (1994). This is a quote by Benedicto Martinez who is a leader in the FAT.
23. This is a quote passed on from a May 1995 interview with Elizabeth Bailey, Editor of *Infrastructure Finance*.
24. See Hayek (1944); Lipset (1959); Friedman (1962); and Bhalla (1995) for basic versions of this neoliberal staple theory.
25. See Chapter 3 for comments by Rimmer de Vries, an institutional investor warning investors of democratization in Chile.
26. 'Mandela's Bond' in *The Economist* (10 December 1994) p. 82.
27. Burns (1995) The first quote is from critics in general. The second is from Ravi Nair, executive director of the South Asian Human Rights Documentation Center based in New Dehli.
28. For an interesting account of how the US limited the IMF's role in constraining Russia policies and encouraged the problem of moral hazard, see Stone (1999).
29. Stone (1999) disagrees with this assertion, on the contrary, he believes that global capital has been the only needed restraint on the over-spending, inflation-inducing policies of Russia. He faults the leniency of the IMF and the US in making loans to Yeltsin.
30. Informal discussion held 17 April 1999 in which David Anderson suggested that he thought it would be better if developing countries did not rely so much on institutional investors and one way to do this would be to increase their domestic savings. Anderson is the head of Citibank's emerging markets investments.

Appendix II

1. I use the rates of change of political rights and civil liberties as my dependent variables rather than political rights and civil liberties rankings because the beginning means for pr and cl are different for emerging and non-emerging countries.
2. I am most interested in the rate of change, and not the overall difference in means. (prrate/clrate = observation 2 − observation 1).
3. This was done because the average rating for political rights and civil liberties was lower in non-emerging market countries.
4. See Przeworski and Limongi (1996) for a good description of the benefits in constructing counterfactuals and using the Heckman selection model to resolve selection bias in comparative political studies.
5. The nefr and emfr variables, report freedom rates for non-emerging and emerging markets respectively but are coded with 'missing' observations for emerging and non-emerging markets freedom rates respectively. This

was done to capture emerging market status within the dependent variable and to enable the use of Stata's Heckman model which performs a probit on the equation of interest's dependent variable to control for the missing observations. This procedure was performed primarily because of Stata software limitations on running a Heckman selection model.

Bibliography

Ahumada, Consuelo (1995) 'The Neoliberal Model and Its Impact on Organized Labor in Colombia: Is Authoritarianism Inherent to the Model?' paper presented at the Annual Meeting of the American Political Science Association, 31 August–3 September.

Anderson, Mark (1998) 'NAFTA on steroids', *Fairfield County Weekly*, June; found on website: http://fairfield weekly.com/articles/mai.html

Andersson, Thomas (1991) *Multinational Investment in Developing Countries*, London & New York: Routledge.

Andrapradesh web site (1999) 'Foreign Investment through GDRs (Euro issues)', website: http://www.andrapradesh.com/laws/ foreigninvestmentthroughgdr.html

Arat, Zehra (1991) *Democracy and Human Rights in Developing Countries*, Boulder, CO: Lynne Rienner Press.

Armijo, Leslie Elliot (1999) 'Mixed Blessings: Expectations about Foreign Capital Flows and Democracy in Emerging Markets' in Armijo, Leslie Elliot (ed.), *Financial Globalization and Democracy in Emerging Markets*, Basingstoke: Macmillan Press – now Palgrave and New York: St. Martin's Press – now Palgrave.

Armour, Lawrence A. and McGowan, Joe (1996) 'A Superstar's Global View: The World According to Barton Biggs', found at *Fortune* web site: http://bubblemouth.pathfinder.com/fortune/19969612223/asi.html

Arrighi, Giovanni (1994) *The Long Twentieth Century*, London: Verso.

Arnold, Wayne (1999) 'More and More Malaysians Question Economic Policies', *New York Times, Late Edition* (4 December), C2.

Balfour, Frederik (1995) 'Vietnam after the Hype', *Institutional Investor*, Vol. 29, Issue 6 (June), 205.

Ball, George (1967) 'The Promise of the MNC', *Fortune*, 75, 6.

Barrineau, James (1997) 'Changing Weights: Positive on Mexico, Taking Chilean Profits', *Smith Barney, Inc. Newsletter*, New York: Smith Barney, 23 June.

Barro, Robert (1994) 'Democracy: A Recipe for Growth?', *Wall Street Journal*, Vol. 224, Issue 107 (1 December), A18 .

Bello, Walden and Rosenfeld, Stephanie (1990) *Dragons in Distress*. San Francisco: Institute for Food and Development Policy.

Bhalla, Surjit (1994) 'Freedom and Economic Growth: A Virtuous Cycle?' in Axel Hadenius (ed.), *Democracy's Victory and Crisis: Nobel Symposium*, Cambridge: Cambridge University Press.

—— (1995) 'Freedom and Economic Growth: A Virtuous Cycle?', in Hadenius, Axel, *Democracy's Victory and Crisis: Nobel Symposium*, Cambridge: Cambridge University Press.

Billet, Bret (1993) *Modernization Theory and Economic Development: Discontent in the Developing World*, Westport, CT: Praeger.

Bloomberg c/o Technimetrics, Inc. (1996), on-line financial services.

Bokhari, Foshan (1999) 'Privatisation on Parade', *The Banker*, vol. 149, Issue 878, April, 6.

Bollen, Kenneth A. (1990) 'Political Democracy: Conceptual and Measurement Traps', *Studies in Comparative International Development*, 25: 7–24.

—— and Jackman, Robert (1985) 'Political Democracy and Size Distribution of Income', *American Sociological Review*, 48, 468–79.

Boorman, Jack (1999) 'Involving the Private Sector in Forestalling and Resolving Financial Crises', speech delivered at IMF press conference (15 April), web site: http://www.imf.org/external/np/tr/1999/TR990415.HTM.

Bourdieu, Pierre (1980) *The Logic of Practice*, Stanford, CA: Stanford University Press.

Burkhart, Ross and Lewis-Beck, Michael S. (1994) 'Comparative Democracy: The Economic Development Thesis', *American Political Science Review*, Vol. 88, no. 4 (December), 903–10.

Burns, John (1995) 'Democracy in India: Now You See It ...' in *New York Times* (22 January), 6.

Business Week (1995) 'Global Investing Can Be a Snake Pit', 138, 11 September.

Bussey, Jane (1998) 'Latin American Finance Ministers Bash New York Credit Rating Agencies', *Knight Ridder/Tribune Business News*, 27 September. Article found at web site: http://web1.infotrac.galegroup.com

Cable, Vincent and Persaud, Bishnodat (1987) *Developing with Foreign Investment*, Kent: Croom-Helm.

Cardosa, Fernando Henrique and Faletto, Enzo (1979) *Dependency and Development in Latin America*, Berkeley: University of California Press.

Cembalest, Michael (1998) 'Morgan Stanley Emerging Market Debt Fund, Inc.', management presentation at Salomon Smith Barney's Eighth Annual Closed-End Funds Conference, 9 April, p. 4.

Central European (1999), 'People', Vol. 9, Issue 6 (July/August), 8–11.

Chernoff, Joel (1999) 'Establishing Guidelines: World Bank and OECD Push Rules', *Pensions & Investments* (28 June), p. 2.

CNNfn (1998) ' "Baby Bras" Hit the Market: Auction of Brazil's Telebras Begins Despite Violent Protests Against the Sale', 29 July, 3:15 pm. ET, web site: http//:europe.cnnfn.com/markets/9807/29/telebras.

Cockburn, Alexander and Silverstein, Ken (1995) 'The Demands of Capital' in *Harper's*, Vol. 290, Issue 1740 (May), 66–7.

Cohen, Bernaud (1996) 'Phoenix Risen: The Resurrection of Global Finance', *World Politics*, 48, 2, January, 269.

Cohen, Youssef (1989) *Manipulation of Consent: The State and Working-class Consciousness in Brazil*, Pittsburgh: University of Pittsburgh Press.

Deyo, Frederic C. (1990) 'Economic Policy and the Popular Sector', in Gereffi, Gary and Wyman, Donald (eds), *Manufacturing Miracles: Paths of Industrialization in Latin America and East Asia*, Princeton: Princeton University Press, 179–204.

Corbridge, Stuart (1993) *Debt and Development*, Oxford, UK and Cambridge, US: Blackwell.

Corporate Board (1996) 'U.S. Investor Activism is Spreading Worldwide', July/August, Vol. 17, Issue 99, 29, 1/3p, web site: http://www.gw4.epnet.com

Cox, Robert (1997) 'The King of Emerging Markets', Templeton Funds web site: www.franklin-templeton.com

Cumings, Bruce (1999) 'The Asian Crisis, Democracy, and the End of Late Development' in T.J. Pempel (ed.), *The Politics of the Asian Economics Crisis*, Ithaca, NY: Cornell University Press.

Dahl, Robert (1971) *Polyachy: Participation and Opposition*, New Haven, CT: Yale University Press.

Daley, Suzanne (1996) 'Few Want Stocks; Now Livestock, That's Different', *New York Times* (8 July), A4.

Devenow, Andrea and Welch, Ivo (1996) 'Rational Herding in Financial Economics', *European Economic Review*, 40-3-5, April, 603–15.

De Vries, Rimmer (1990) 'Foreign Direct Investment in Heavily Indebted Developing Countries: A View from the Financial Community' in Cynthia Day Wallace (ed.), Foreign Direct Investment in the 1990s: A New Climate in the Third World, The Netherlands: Martinus Nijhoff.

Diamond, Douglas and Verrecchia Robert E. (1981) 'Information Aggregation in a Noisy Rational Expectations Model', *Journal of Financial Economics*, 9(3), 221–36.

Dornbusch, R. (1998) 'A Model of Confusion: Soros Lacks the Clarity of Thought for His Vast Agenda', *Financial Times*, 19 December; found at web site: http://www.globalarchrive.ft.com

Doherty, Jaqueline (1998) 'World Bank's Treasury: A Force in the Market', *Barron's* (25 May), 30.

Dow Jones News (1996), 'GT Natural Resources – Uses 'Cockroach Theory' for Exits', 16 October: Subject: MUTF USA.

Drucker, Peter (1991) 'Reckoning with the Pension Fund Revolution' in *Harvard Business Review*, (March–April), 106–14.

Echeverri-Gent, John (1999) 'India: Financial Globalization, Liberal Norms, and the Ambiguities of Democracy' in Leslie Elliott Armijo (ed.), *Financial Globalization and Democracy in Emerging Markets*, Basingstoke: Macmillan Press – now Palgrave and New York: St. Martin's Press – now Palgrave 207–32.

The Economist (1999) 351 'Getting Hostile', Issue 8120 (22 May): 2–5.

Eichengreen, Barry (1999) 'Toward a New International Financial Architecture: A Practical Post-Asia Agenda', February (Washington, DC: Institute for International Finance). Web site http://pbs.org/wgbh/pages/frontline/shows/crash/solutions.

Elizondo, Carlos Mayer-Serra (1999) 'Mexico: Foreign Investment and Democracy' in Leslie Elliott Armijo (ed), *Financial Globalization and Democracy in Emerging Markets*, Basingstoke: Macmillan Press – now Palgrave and New York: St. Martin's Press – Palgrave), pp. 117–30.

Emerging Market Traders' Association (1995) *Annual Report.*

Eng, Maximo V., Lees, Francis A. and Mauer, Laurence J. (1998) *Global Finance*, Reading, MA: Addison-Wesley.

Errunza, V.F. and Rosenberg, Barr (1982) 'Investment in Developed and Less Developed Countries,' *Journal of Financial and Quantitative Analysis*, (December): 753–5

——European Institute for Asia Studies (1998) 'The Asian Crisis and the World: Risks and Opportunities', Roundtable Discussion, October; summary of presentations found at: http://www.eias.org/main pages/EIAS/ Seminars/Ell Asia relations intimesof crisis/Roundtable/1/20/99. html

Evans Peter (1979) *Dependent Development: The Alliance of Multinational, State and Local Capital in Brazil*, Princeton: Princeton University Press.

——(1987) 'Foreign Capital and the Third World State' in Huntington, Samuel and Wiener, Myron (eds), *Understanding Political Development*, Boston: Little, Brown and Company.

Faison, Seth (1997) 'Hong Kong Stocks Fall Steeply: New Victim of Region's Ills', *Wall Street Journal* (23 October), D1+.

Feldstein, Martin (1995) 'Too Little, Not Too Much', *The Economist* (24 June); 72–3.

——and Horioka Charles, (1980) 'Domestic Savings and International Capital Flows', *Economic Journal*.

Fernandez-Kelly, Patricia (1983) *For We Are Sold, I and My People: Women and Industry in Mexicos Frontier*, Albany: State University of New York Press.

Financial Times (1998) 'Rainbow Loses Its Shine as Woes Accumulate: Following the Achievement of Its Political Miracle, the ANC Government Is Now Being Called On To Work New Wonders,' (21 October), 2, web site: http:www.globalarchive.ft.com.search/FTJSPController.html

Fisher, Klaus and Papaioannou, George (1992) *Business Finance in Less Developed Capital Markets*, Westport CT: Greenwood Press.

Fisher and Sobokin (1995)

Fosback, Norman G. (1995) *Stock Market Logic*, Dearborn, MI: Dearborn Financial Publishing, Inc.

Foucault, Michel (1979) *Discipline and Punish*, New York: Vintage Books.

Fraga (1996)

Frieden, Jeffry (1987) *Banking on the World*, New York: Harper & Row.

——(1991) 'Invested Interests,' *International Organization*, 45, 4 (Autumn), 425–51.

——(1981) 'Third World Indebted Industrialization: International Finance and State Capitalism in Mexico, Brazil, Algeria and South Korea', *International Organization*, vol. 35, no. 3, 407–31.

Friedman, Milton (1962) *Capitalism and Freedom*, Chicago: University of Chicago Press.

Friedman, Thomas (1999) *The Lexus and the Olive Tree*, New York: Farrar, Strauss, Giroux.

Froebel, Golker, Heinrichs, Jorgen and Kreye, Otto (1981) *The International Division of Labour*, New York: Cambridge University Press.

Garber, Peter (1990) 'Famous First Bubbles', *Journal of Economic Perspectives*, 4(2), 35–42.

Garrett, Geoffrey (1998) 'External Risk and Domestic Compensation in Developing Countries,' paper presented at the APSA Annual Meeting, Boston, 3 September.

Gasiorowski Mark (1994) 'Economic Crisis and Political Regime Change: An Event History Analysis', paper presented at the American Political Science Association Confernce, 2 September.

Gasparino, Charles (1996) 'Hot Emerging-Bond Funds Leave Some Investors Cold', *Wall Street Journal*, reprinted by NewsEdge, Dow Jones and Company, 6 November.

Gastil, Raymond D. (1987) *Freedom in the World*. New York: Freedom House.

George, Robert Lloyd (1993) *A Handbook of Emerging Markets*, Chicago, IL and Cambridge, UK: Probus Publishing.

Gilpin, Robert (1974) *U.S. Power and the Multinational Corporation: The Political Economy of Foreign Direct Investment*, New York: Simon & Schuster.

Glasgall, William (1995) 'The Currency Casualty List Could Get a Lot Longer', *Business Week*, 16 January 48–55.

Glen, Jack and Pinto, Brian (1994) 'Emerging Capital Markets and Corporate Finance' in *The Columbia Journal of World Business*, Summer.

Glover, David and Tussie, Diana (ed). (1993) *The Developing Countries in World Trade: Policies and Bargaining Strategies*, Boulder, CO: Lynne Rienner.

Gopinath, Deepak (1999) 'Now Comes the Politics', *Institutional Investor*, vol. 33, Issue 3, March, 81.

Gonick, Lev and Rosh, Robert M. (1988) 'The Structural Constraints of the World-Economy on National Political Development', *Comparative Political Studies*, 21, 171–99.

Graham, Edward and Krugman, Paul R. (1993) 'The Surge in Foreign Direct Investment in the 1980s', National Bureau of Economic Research Project, Report, Chicago and London: University of Chicago Press.

Gramsci, Antonio (1971) *Selections from Prison Notebooks*, New York: International Publishers.

Gray, John (1999) *False Dawn: The Delusions of Global Capitalism*, New York: The New Press.

Grossman, Sanford J. and Stiglitz, Joseph E. (1976) 'Information and Competitive Prices Systems,' *American Economic Review*, 66(2), 246–53.

Gurria, Jose Angel (1998) Address to the Economic Club of New York, 11 March, reprinted on web site: http://www.chcp.gob.mx/english/docs/pr980312.html

Gustafson, Lowell (1995) 'Privatization and Oligarchy in Argentina', paper presented at the American Political Science Association's Annual Meeting, Chicago.

Haggard, Stephen (1990) *Pathways from the Periphery: The Politics of Growth in the Newly Industrialized Countries*, Ithaca: Cornell University Press.

——and Steven Webb (eds) (1994) *Voting for Reform*. Oxford: Oxford University Press.

Haggard, Stephen, Kaufman, Robert and Webb, Stephen (1990) 'Politics Inflation and stabilization in Middle Income Countries'; World Bank Working Paper, September.

Hansen-Kuhn, Karen (1997) 'Privatization in Mexico: Telmex', *The Development GAP* (April); reprinted on web site: http://www.50years.org. factsheets/telmex/html, pp. 1–3.

Hardouvelis, Gikas, La Porta, Rafael and Wizman, Thierry (1994) 'What Moves the Discount on Country Equity Funds?' in Jeffrey A. Frankel (ed.), *Internationalization of Equity Markets* (Cambridge, MA: National Bureau of Economic Research (NBER)), 345–97.

Hartmann, Mark and Khambata, Dara (1993) 'Emerging Stock Markets', *The Columbia Journal of World Business*, 29(2) (Summer), 83–103.

Harvey, David (1989) *The Condition of Postmodernity*, Oxford, UK: Blackwell and Cambridge, MA.

Hayek, Friedrich (1944) *The Road to Serfdom*. Chicago, IL: University of Chicago Press.

Heilbrunn, John (1995) 'Elites, Economic Reform, and Political Liberalization in Francophone Africa', paper presented at the Annual Meeting of the Political Science Association, Chicago, IL, 29 August–3 September.

Herbst, Jeffrey and Adebayo Olukoshi (1994) 'Nigeria: Economic and Political Reforms at Cross Purposes' in Stephen Haggard and Steven Webb (eds), *Voting for Reform*, Oxford: Oxford University Press.

Hirsch, James S. (1996) 'Treasure Hunters – Exotic Markets Beckon Again' *Wall Street Journal Interactive* edition (12 November), 1–2.

Hirschman, Albert (1970) *Exit, Voice, and Loyalty*, Cambridge: Cambridge University Press.

Hirst, Paul and Zeitlin, Jonathan (1991) 'Flexible Specialization Versus Post Fordism: Theory, Evidence and Policy Implications', *Economy and Society*, 20, 1–56.

Howell, Michael J. (1995) 'Institutional Investors and Emerging Stock Markets' in Stijn Claessens and Sudarshan Goopta (eds), *Portfolio Investment in Developing Countries*, Washington, DC: World Bank.

Huntington, Samuel P. (1968) *Political Order in Changing Societies*, New Haven, ET: Yale University Press.

IIF (Institute of International Finance) (1999) 'Global Private Finance Leaders Stress the Importance of Voluntary Approaches to Crisis Resolution in Emerging Markets', Press release, web site: http://www.iif.com/pressrel/1999pr9.html

IFC (International Finance Corporation). (1999) *Emerging Markets Database*.

—— (1995) *Emerging Stock Markets Yearbook*.

—— (1996a) *Emerging Stock Markets Factbook*.

—— (1996b) *Monthly Review of Emerging Stock Markets*, May.

—— (1996c) *Quarterly Review of Emerging Markets*.

IMF (International Monetary Fund). (1998). 'World Economic Outlook and International Capital Markets: Interim Assessment', December, Washington, DC: IMF.

—— (1994) *Balance of Payment Statistics Yearbook*.

—— (1995) *Private Market Financing for Developing Countries*.

Jabine, Thomas and Richard Claude (eds) (1992) *Human Rights and Statistics: Getting the Record Straight*. Philadelphia: University of Pennsylvania Press.

Javetski, Bill and William Glasgall (1995) 'Borderless Finance: Fuel for Growth', *Business Week* (24 January), 40–50.

Jebb, Fiona (1995) 'The Challenges of Economic Change' in Knobel, Lance (ed.), *New World Business*, London: Euromoney Publications and Worldlink, 8–10.

Johnson, Robert (1999) Interview from 'The Crash' broadcast on PBS *Frontline*. Transcript available on website: http://www.pbs.org/wgbh/pages/frontline/shows/crash/interviews/johnson.html

Kijima, Kazuo (1996) Personal correspondence with Shoken Toshishintaku Kyokai, Toyko, Japan.

Kingstone, Peter (1999) 'Brazil: Short on Foreign Money, Long Domestic Political Cycles' in Armijo, Leslie Elliott (ed.), *Financial Globalization and Democracy in Emerging Markets*, Basingstoke: Macmillan Press – now Palgrave and New York: St. Martin's Press – now Palgrave, 151–76.

Klebnikov, Paul, 'Emerging Markets After the Crash,' *Forbes*, vol. 155, 19 June, 186.

Kmenta, J. (1986) *Elements of Econometrics*, 2nd edn., New York: Macmillan.

Kraus, James R. (1999) 'Bankers Fight G-7 proposals to Revamp Poor Nation's Debt,' *American Banker*, 164(121) 25 June, 1.

Krugman, Paul (1995) 'Dutch Tulips and the Emerging Markets', *Foreign Affairs* (July), Vol. 74, 4.

Kuczynski, Pedro-Pablo (1994) 'Why Emerging Markets?' in *The Columbia Journal of World Business* (Summer), 9–13.

Kumar, P.C. (1994) 'Inefficiencies from Financial Liberalization in the Absence of Well-Functioning Equity Markets' in *Journal of Money, Credit, and Banking*, 26(2), May, 341–4.

Lash, Scott and Urry John, (1994) *The Economies of Signs and Space*, London: Sage Publications.

Lee, Shelley A. (1995) 'A World of Opportunity', *Pension Management*, 31 (6) (June), 14–33.

Lehner, Urban (1997) 'Money Hungry', *Wall Street Journal*, 19 September, R1–R28.

Lipset, Seymour Martin (1959) 'Some Social Requisites of Democracy: Economic Development and Political Legitimacy', *American Political Science Review*, 53, 69–105.

Lissakers, Karin (1991) *Banks, Borrowers, and the Establishment: A Revisionist Account of the International Debt Crisis*, New York: Basic Books.

McLeod, Darryl and Welch, John H. (1991) 'North American Free Trade and the Peso', Federal Reserve Bank of Dallas Working Paper, no. 9115.

Mader, Chris and Hagin, Robert (1976) *Dow Jones – Irwin Guide to Common Stocks*, Homewood, IL: Dow Jones-Irwin.

Mahathir, Mohamed (1997) 'Asian Economies', reprinted in *Vital Speeches of the Day*, 15 October 1997. Delivered at the Annual Seminar of the World Bank in Hong Kong, 20 Semptember (1994) Vol. 64, Issue 1, 9.

Makin, Claire (1992) 'Hard-won Wisdom on Emerging Markets', *Institutional Investor* (September), 183–7.

Malas, Iyad (1995) 'Key Trends in Emerging Stock Markets in 1993' in Lance Knobel (ed.), *New World Business,* (London: Euromoney Publications and Worldlink); pp. 23–5.

Malkiel, Burton G. (1982) *The Inflation Beater's Investment Guide,* New York: W.W. Norton.

——(1973) *A Random Walk Down Wall Street.* New York: W.W. Norton.

Malpass, David (1997) *CNBC Broadcast* (13 May), 3.25 pm.

Mainwaring, Scott (1993) 'Presidentialism, Multipartyism and Democracy: The Difficult Combination; Comparative Political Studies 26, 198–228.

'Mandela's Bond', *The Economist* (10 December), 82.

Manzocchi, Stefano (1999) 'Capital Flows to Developing Economies throughout the Twentieth Century' in Armijo, Leslie Elliot (ed.), *Financial Globalization and Democracy in Emerging Markets,* Basingstoke, UK: Macmillan Press – now Palgrave and New York: St. Martin's Press, 51–73.

Marotta, George (1996) 'Global Investing Is Enticing but Risky: Consider a Portfolio Allocation that Matches World Market Capitalization', *It's Your Money* (New York: BRIDGE news) 9/11.

Maxfield, Sylvia and Hoffman, Joshua (1995) 'International Portfolio Flows to Developing/Transitional Economies: Impact on Government Policy Choice', paper presented at the Workshop on 'Financial Globalization and Emerging Markets: Policy Autonomy, Democratization and the Lessons from Mexico', Watson Institute of International Studies, Brown University, 18–19 November.

Mckinnon, Ronald I. (1995) 'Flood of Dollars, Sunken Pesos', *New York Times,* 20 Jannary, A29.

McTague, Jim (1998) 'It's a New World: An Aussie-born Wall Street Veteran Shakes Up a Big Multinational Lender', *Barron's* (25 May), 27–31.

Melloan, George (1996) 'Global View: Bill Clinton's Second-Term Scylla and Charybdis', *Wall Street Journal* (11 November), A17.

Mellow, Craig (1998) 'The Man Who Was Emerging Markets', *Institutional Investor International Edition,* Vol. 23, Issue 10 (October), 48.

Meyer, Robert L. and Andy B. Skov (1999) 'Emerging Markets Portfolio Overview' in *Morgan Stanley Dean Witter Institutional Fund, Inc. Annual Report* (January), 24–9.

Middle East Economic Digest (1999) 'Turkish Market Soars on IMF News', 30 June, 28.

Mobius, Mark (1995) *The Investor's Guide to Emerging Markets.* Burr Ridge, IL and New York, New York: Irwin Publishing.

——(1996) *Mobius on Emerging Markets,* London: Pitman Publishing.

Mody, Ashoka and Michael Walton (1998) 'Building on East Asia's Infrastructure Foundations', *Finance and Development* (June), Vol. 35, No. 2, 22–5.

Molano, Walter (1995) 'From Bad Debts to Healthy Securities? The Theory and Financial Techniques of the Brady Plan', paper presented at the Workshop on 'Financial Globalization and Emerging Markets: Policy Autonomy, Democratization and the Lessons from Mexico',

Watson Institute of International Studies, Brown University, 18–19 November.

Moran, Theodor (ed.) (1986) *Investing in Development: New Roles for Private Capital?*, Washington, DC: Overseas Development Council.

Morles, Gustavo (1996) 'The Mexican Crisis and the Latin American Debt Redux', *Center for Latin American Capital Markets Research* (January).

Moshavi, Sharon and Engardio, Pete (1995) 'India Shakes Off Its Shackles', *Business Week* (30 January), 48.

Muehring, Kevin (1995) 'Can They Really Build a New Monetary Order?', *Institutional Investor* Vol. 29/6 (June), 37–42.

Nameth, Louise (1993) 'Development Banks Search for a New Direction' in *Infrastructure Finance* (autumn), 18.

Norton, Rob (1997) 'George Soros: Billionaire, Genius, Fool', *Fortune*, 17 March; found on web site: http://www.pathfinder.com/@@258874AcA67 NhmbWI/Fortune/1997/970317/rea.html

Ohmae, Kenichi (1995) 'Putting Global Logic First', *Harvard Business Review*, 73/1 (January–February), 119–125.

Nelson, Joan (1990) *Economic Crisis and Policy Choice*, Princeton, NJ: Princeton University Press.

Olson, Mancur (1994) 'Dictatorship, Democracy, and Development', *American Political Science Review* (September).

Payer, Cheryl (1991) *Lent and Lost: Foreign Credit and Third World Development*, London: Zed Books.

Bresser Pereira, Luiz Carlos (1993) 'Economic Reforms and Economic Growth: Efficiency and Politics in Latin America', in Bresser Pereira, Luiz Carlos, Maravall, Jose Maria and Przewoiski, Adam (eds), *Economic Reforms in New Democracies: A Social Democratic Approach*, Cambridge: Cambridge University Press.

Perry, Christopher (1994) 'Hot New Funds Look for High Yields', *Infrastructure Finance*, 3(3)(June/July), 19–24.

Pennar, Karen (1995) 'Why Investors Stampede', *Business Week*, 13 February, 84–5.

Pion-Berlin, David (1989) *The Ideology of State Terror: Economic Doctrine and Political Repression in Argentina and Peru.* Boulder, CO: Lynne Rienner.

Political Risk Services (1995) Web address: Polrisk@aol.com

Polyani, Karl (1957) *The Great Transformation: The Political and Economic Origins of Our Time*, Boston: Beacon Books.

Porter, Tony (1999) 'Transitional Agenda for Financial Regulation in Developing Countries', in Armijo, Leslie Elliott (ed.), *Financial Globalization and Democracy in Emerging Markets.*

Prochniak, Andrea (1996) 'Playing Emerging Markets', *Forbes*, 133/6 (April), 154.

Przeworski, Adam (1991) *Democracy and the Market: Political and Economic Reforms in Eastern Europe and Latin America*, Cambridge: Cambridge University Press.

Przeworski, Adam and Limongi, Fernando (1996) 'Selection, Counterfactuals, and Comparisons' unpublished paper.

——Pereira, Luiz Carlos Bresser and Maravall, Jose (eds) (1993) *Economic Reforms in New Democracies: A Social Democratic Approach*, (Cambridge: Cambridge University Press).

Rademan, Chad (1996) 'Just How Good Are Emerging-Markets Indexes?', *Institutional Invester*, June, 82–7.

Remmer, Karen (1986) 'The Politics of Economic Stabilization: IMF Standby Programs in Latin America, 1954–1984', *Comparative Politics*, 19 October.

——(1989) *Military Rule in Latin America*, Boston: Unwin Hyman.

——(1990) 'Democracy and Econimic Crisis: The Latin American Experience', *World Politics*, 4,2,3, April.

Reuters Money Network. (1996) Research database on CD-Rom.

Romero, Simon (1999) 'Brazil: Banks Profited from Devaluation', *New York Times*, 26 March, reprinted at http://igc.org/trac/corner/worldnews/other/336.html

Rosenn, Keith S. (1991) *Foreign Investment in Brazil*, Boulder, CO: Westview Press.

Rubin, Robert (1998) 'Restoring Global Financial Stability', remarks at Yale University Law School, (New Haven, CT), 17 October.

Sanger, David E. (1999) 'U.S. and IMF Warn Brazil Not to Try and Prop Up Currency', *New York Times* (15 January), C1–C4.

Schemo, Diana Jean (1997) 'Peruvian Rebels Urge Fujimori to Resume Hostage Talks', *New York Times* (5 January), 8.

Sender, Henny (1995) 'Riding High', *Far Eastern Economic Review*, Vol. 158, No. 21 (25 May), 66.

Sesit, Michael (1997) 'Global Investors Depend on Invisible Force: The Custodian', *Wall Street Journal Interactive* edition, 26 June. web site: http://update.wsj.com/public/current/articles/SB867078288222704500.htm.

Schwab, Klaus and Claude Smadja (1994) 'Power and Policy: the New Economic World Order' in *Harvard Business Review*, 72/6 (November–December), 40–50.

Shameen, Assif (1996) 'Still Fizz Left in Wall Street: But Asia Should Benefit When It Turns Flat', in *Asiaweek* (23 August) 1–4, web site: www.pathfinder.com/asiaweek/96/0823/bi6.html

Shari, Michael (1996) 'The Stampede to Finance Indonesia Inc.', *Business Week*, N3467 (18 March), 107.

Sims, Calvin (1997) 'Hostage Crisis Imperils the Growth of Peru's Economy', *New York Times* (5 January), 8.

Sklair, Leslie (1991) *Sociology of the Global System*, Baltimore: Johns Hopkins University Press.

Smith, Geri and Malkin, Elisabeth (1995) 'Mexico: Can it Cope?', *Business Week*, Issue 3407 (16 January), 42–7.

Sobel, Andrew (1997) 'The Command and Former Command Economies in Global Financial Markets', paper presented at the Midwest Political Science Association Conference, Chicago, IL.

Solomon, Steven (1995) *The Confidence Game*, New York: Simon & Schuster.

Soros, George (1998–99) 'Capitalism's Last Chance', *Foreign Policy* (Winter); found on web site: http://foreignpolicy.com

South Africa Investor (1995) 'South Africa Moves into U.S. Institutional Portfolios', Washington, DC: Investor Responsibility Research Center, 9–10 January.

Spragins, Ellyn E. and McGinn, Daniel (1995) 'Spanning the Globe', *Newsweek*, 125/155.7 (13 February), 52.

Stiglitz, Joseph (1999) as quoted in 'World Bank Bigwig Blames Economists for Bad Advice', *Dollars and Sense*, 224 (July/August) 8–9.

Stone, Randall (1999) 'Russia: The IMF, Private Finance, and External Constraints on a Fragile Polity' in Leslie Elliott Armijo (ed.), *Financial Globalization and Democracy in Emerging Markets*, Basingstoke: Macmillan Press – now Palgrave and New York: St. Martin's Press – now Palgrave 177–206.

Strange, Susan (1997) *Casino Capitalism*, 2nd ed, Manchester, UK and New York: Manchester University Press.

Tesar, Linda and Werner Ingrid, (1993) 'US Equity Investment in Emerging Stock Markets' in Claessens, Stijn and Goopta, Sudarshan (eds), *Portfolio Investment in Developing Countries*, Washington, DC: The World Bank.

Trustnet (1996) Web site for unit trust information at http://www.trustnet.com, London.

Unger, David (1999) 'Thailand: What Goes Up ... ' in Armijo, Leslie Elliott (ed.), *Financial Globalization and Democracy in the Emerging Markets*, Basingstoke: Macmillan and New York: St. Martin's Press – now Palgrave, 276–98.

Useem, Michael (1996) *Investor Capitalism*, New York: Basic Books.

Wachtel, Howard (1986) *The Money Mandarins*, New York: Pantheon Books.

Wallace, Cynthia Day (1990) *Foreign Direct Investment in the 1990's: A New Climate in the Third World*, The Netherlands: Martinus Nijhoff Publishers.

Wedel, Janine R. (1998) 'The Harvard Boys Do Russia', *The Nation*, Vol. 266, no. 20 (1 June) 11–16.

Weisbrot, Mark (1999) 'Neoliberalism Comes Unglued'. Mark Weisbrot is Research Director at the Preamble Center, in Washington, DC www.preamble.org

Welch, Ivo, Hirshleifer, David and Bikhchandani, Sushil (1992) 'A Theory of Fads, Fashion, Custom and Cultural Change as Informational Cascade', *Journal of Political Economy*, 100, 5, October, 992–1026.

Wessel, David (1997) 'Developing Nations Require Open Markets', *Wall Street Journal* (15 September), 1.

Williamson, John, (1990) *Latin American Adjustment: How Much Has Happened?*, Washington, DC: Institute for International Economics.

——(1994) 'The Political Economy of Policy Reform,' *Institute for International Economics*, Washington, DC.

Winters, Jeffrey A. (1999) 'Indonesia: On the Mostly Negative Role of Transnational Capital in Democratization' in Leslie Elliott Armijo (ed.), *Financial Globalization and Democracy in Emerging Markets*, Basingstoke: Macmillan Press – now Palgrave and New York: St. Martin's Press, 233–50.

Wolf, Holger C. (1998) 'Is There a Curse of Location?: Spatial Determinants of Capital Flows to Emerging Markets', *NBER Reporter,* Spring Issue 0276-119X, 38.

World Bank (1999) *Global Development Finance* on CD-ROM.

Zimmerman, Robert (1993) *Dollars, Diplomacy and Dependency: Dilemmas in U.S. Economic Aid,* Boulder, CO: Lynne Rienner.

Index